Questions

The Islamic Space

Questions

A series of explorations by
William Corlett & John Moore

WILLIAM CORLETT
&
JOHN MOORE

The Islamic Space

HAMISH HAMILTON
LONDON

First published in Great Britain 1979 by
Hamish Hamilton Ltd., Garden House, 57–59 Long Acre
London WC2E 9JZ

ISBN 0 241 10007 0

The authors and publisher are indebted to the following for the use of copyright material: Routledge & Kegan Paul, Ltd., London, and Samuel Weiser Inc. for permission to quote from *The Conference of the Birds* by Farid ud-Din Attar, translated by C. S. Knott; Penguin Books Ltd., London, for permission to quote from *The Koran*, translated by N. J. Dawood, © N. J. Dawood 1956, 1959, 1966, 1968, 1974; J. M. Dent & Sons Ltd., London, for permission to quote from *The Koran*, translated by J. M. Rodwell (Everyman's Library); Sh. Muhammad Ashraf, Lahore, for permission to quote from *The Persian Mystics: Rumi*, by F. Hadland Davis.

Printed in Great Britain by
Ebenezer Baylis and Son Ltd.
The Trinity Press, Worcester, and London

This book is one of a series.

The titles are *The Question of Religion*, *The Christ Story*, *The Hindu Sound*, *The Judaic Law*, *The Buddha Way* and *The Islamic Space*. The books were written in the order as listed, but this in no way implies any suggested precedence of one religion over another, nor any preference on the part of the authors. Each book may be read in its own right, rather as each note of an octave may sound alone.

However, for an octave to be complete, it depends on the developing frequency and character of each note. In the same way, it has been the experience of the authors, approaching this series as one work, to find a similar development as they progressed from one book to another.

. . . the flight of the unknown to the unknown . . .

Part One

O my heart, if you wish to arrive at the beginning of understanding, walk carefully. To each atom there is a different door, and for each atom there is a different way which leads to the mysterious Being of whom I speak. To know oneself one must live a hundred lives. But you must know God by Himself and not by you; it is He who opens the way that leads to Him, not human wisdom. The knowledge of Him is not at the door of rhetoricians. Knowledge and ignorance are here the same, for they cannot explain nor can they describe. The opinions of men on this arise only in their imagination; and it is absurd to try to deduce anything from what they say: whether ill or well, they have said it from themselves. God is above knowledge and beyond evidence, and nothing can give an idea of His Holy Majesty.

(*The Conference of the Birds*, Farid ud-Din Attar)

*

To those people who are familiar with religion only as dogmatic belief and ritual performance these words will seem strange and perhaps even heretical. Nevertheless they derive from the mysterious, esoteric tradition of Islam and they will serve to introduce the theme of this book.

Of course, such mystery is not unique to Islam. Behind their outward presentation to the world, all the great religious traditions have scriptures of an equally enigmatic nature. However, we—the authors of this book which is one of a series—have come to a point, or an interval, in our writing, which happens to coincide with consideration of the Islamic tradition. Here we find that we have no option but to suggest that anyone who questions the mystery of his own existence will inevitably come to this mysterious threshold across which the concepts, beliefs and logical explanations of the human mind will not carry him.

From here onwards only his individual understanding will suffice.

*

But you must know God by Himself and not by you.

II

Islam:
The word means "surrender" or "submission".
By whom or what?
To whom or what?

*

Space:
That which appears to be between one and another.
What space is there between Man and God?

*

Questions:
The means by which Man seeks to resolve his apparent aloneness, incompleteness and ignorance.

The means by which he "surrenders" to the realization that "space" is an illusion created by his own mind.

When all the explanations and performances of the world have come to nothing, there only remains the "mysterious journey" or The Quest, as each of us inevitably fulfils his destiny—an experience sometimes called "the flight of the unknown to the unknown".

*

A strange beginning? An absurd beginning? A meaningless beginning? A challenging beginning?
Who is to say?
Only you.

*

A*   3

Every book has a manifest beginning.

There is a beginning for the writer and a beginning for the reader.

Thousands of words pass as thought-forms through the writer's mind and he selects those which seem most accurately to express what he wants to say. This selection is put in writing on the blank sheet of paper before him.

For the reader, the beginning is the first word of the finished book. As he begins to read, he selects from his memory his interpretation of the meaning of the words.

*

The writer begins with the desire to select words which will express as clearly as possible some idea, feeling, concept, belief, opinion, question, problem, or whatever. He desires to express something in order to communicate—to an unknown reader.

The reader begins by acquiring the book and opens it in anticipation. Of what? Of satisfying some desire? Perhaps a desire associated with his own aloneness, incompleteness or ignorance? It may be that he hopes to discover a helpful idea, a promising concept, a sympathetic belief, a confirming opinion, a common problem, his own question, a possible answer, or whatever.

Thus the communication between writer and reader is attempted —expressed by one, interpreted by the other. The time and space between us is eliminated in the immediacy of these words, here and now. The words of our attempted communication must depend on the honesty and willingness of both to admit our common purpose.

This book, as with the others in the series, does not attempt to give conclusive answers. On the contrary it will ask many questions. The purpose of this is to convey that, "beneath" our worldly concerns and diversions, we all harbour our sense of aloneness, incompleteness and ignorance. If we can but admit that, then we are on the threshold of truly religious aspiration, the mystical journey . . . together. We just may give each other the courage to set out on that journey.

*

The knowledge of Him is not at the door of rhetoricians. Knowledge and ignorance are here the same, for they cannot explain nor can they describe. The opinions of men on this arise only in their imagination; and it is absurd to try to deduce anything from what they say: whether ill or well, they have said it from themselves . . .

*

And so, as we speak of our enquiry, here in the context of Islam, we find great mystery as we each attempt to penetrate the depths of our understanding.

Whether we choose to suppress or ignore them, or otherwise divert our attention from their presence, the human mind entertains such questions as:

Who am I?

Where did I come from?

What is the purpose of my existence?

What happens when I die?

Why this universe?

How was it created?

What does the universe mean to me?

What am I to this universe?

*

And of particular concern if I am religious:

Is there an almighty God—are there gods?

*

Like millions of aspirants before us, we hear these questions and we endeavour to respond to them. We experience in our minds the desire to know the answers to them. Perhaps we find them daunting, even overwhelming. Perhaps we take up their challenge and we embark upon a search for the answers. Naturally, at first, we consult the words of those held to be wise, both from the past and in the present. Conditioning and learning lead us to believe that the answers are "out there", somewhere hidden in the annals of worldly wisdom or available for the asking from contemporary wise men if only we can find them.

But, curiously, there is one thing that we usually do not do; we do not pause to consider the questioning itself.

What *is* a question?

Where does it come from?

Who is asking it?

"I am," we would assuredly answer.

The question manifests in *my* mind and it is thought and formulated in *my* mind. It may then be asked by *my* voice.

But who put it into my mind?

Who is *really* asking the question that I am experiencing?

*

We do not have questions when we are born.

We do not even consciously question the fact that we have come to exist.

We are here, and that is that.

During the early years we experience our environment through the medium of our bodies but we have no concept of the world nor of ourselves as being separate from the world.

We simply accept what is. We do not know that we are potential human adults; we are unknown to ourselves.

We eat, drink and sleep, unaware of the phenomenon of our existence, unaware of ourselves as separate, unaware of any questions.

Then we learn language and we are told many facts about the world and the nature of human life. We are taught to survive.

It is then that my mind conceives the idea that "I am separate." It is *my* survival that becomes apparent . . . along with the survival of all the other millions of particular human beings.

In this process, we take much for granted. We do not have the power to do otherwise. Innocently, we accept the facts we are given and understand them to be the truth. My idea of who and what I

6

am is conditioned by the circumstances of the time and place of the birth and upbringing of my body.

*

Eventually, apart from the many practical facts of life, I become aware of a phenomenon called "religion".

Among the manifold activities of man—all the pre-occupation with survival and pleasure—there is this mysterious area of human concern where people perform strange rituals, often in certain buildings set aside for the purpose. In these special circumstances, the nature of behaviour is quite different.

What is going on?

Outside, all is competition to survive and succeed; inside, all this ceases.

*

It transpires later, as my learning and experience evolves, that man's unique ability to be conscious of his own existence poses considerable problems. For example, he is able to know that he will die.

For all his considerable accumulation of knowledge about the physical world and his ability to survive in it to better effect than any other creature, man's intelligence is also capable of probing metaphysical realms where "facts" are hard to come by. In this realm he is far less secure and it may not be at all comfortable.

I begin to become aware of the strange and unsubstantial world of other men's ideas, beliefs and opinions about life and death. It is a challenging and perplexing world of assertion and doubt—and dubious evidence. Unlike, say, the accepted fact of existence that the body needs food to maintain its life, here is a situation where one man's theory can be used to condition himself and influence another, perhaps even me.

Why should any man want me to believe what he believes?

*

Man becomes aware of the mystery of his own existence.

Arising from this consciousness, there enter his mind such questions as, "Who created this universe and why?"

Due to the development of human language and the ability to transpose the spoken word into written hieroglyphs, we learn that such questions have challenged man for thousands of years. Although he displays much confidence in himself to combat threats to his physical survival, man has always been aware that his activities are very much subject to natural laws and are circumscribed by factors out of his control. His will is limited in its scope. The social structures he has devised are precarious and are continually being undermined. He is proved vulnerable over and over again. Hence his continuing endeavour to resist the limitations and his attempts to resolve the fears which they give rise to. For all that, such people realize and admit that man's knowledge and will pales into insignificance when compared with what he does not know and cannot will.

In acknowledgement and deference to the "unknown" which circumscribes the limited sphere in which he exercises what he calls "his will", man has always allowed that there could be, or must be, intelligence and power superior to his own.

Having accepted this, then there is no option but to consider himself subject to that which he believes superior to himself.

Hence, religion. Hence, the mysterious area of human concern. Hence, the strange rituals in the religious places set apart for the purpose. Hence, the change in the nature of behaviour in these special circumstances.

In a situation where he is acknowledging an intelligence and power superior to his own, his worldly strivings naturally cease.

The problem is—and always has been—how to conceive of That to which he is subject?

*

History tells us that different people in different places have conceptualized the superior intelligence or power in widely varying

8

ways. And, of course, they have done it within the circumstances in which they have found themselves and in their own form of language and expression.

It may interest us to study these various schools of belief and the ways in which they have expressed what they have discovered and claimed to have understood.

Why should we do this?

To see to what extent they succeeded?

How could we judge?

And even if we decided they had succeeded, would that be of any value to us?

Only if we found we could adopt and believe their way?

Could we really and truly do that?

*

But you must know God by Himself and not by you . . .

*

One of the key features which has emerged from man's contemplation of these matters—his "religious aspiration"—is that through our experience of being aware that we are here (knowing we exist) and through our observation that every object and event is governed by law, we conceive the idea that "something caused" us and the universe to exist (and causes us and the universe to continue to exist).

Also, through our comprehension and experience of law, we have conceived of number and sequence. We have learned to begin with what we have called "one", the "first". This is derived from the fact that we can conceive of the whole, the totality, of everything. The totality cannot be other than singular and unified. From one, all else, all other numbers, follow. What is more, all that follows must be derived from the one. If the conception of one is valid, there cannot be two of them.

This is very simple, and easily taken for granted. It is miraculous that the human mind can conceive of a unified totality. The

9

difficulty is to hold the concept in its purity—and it is this that has bedevilled theological debate through the ages.

For it is natural and appropriate for the concept to evolve that the "something" which caused us and the universe (meaning "turned or combined into one") must itself be the first and single factor superior to all else.

Ever since, in the distant past of human psychology, the first proposition of a unique, causal factor, it has been the concern of men to attempt to discover how to comprehend and relate to it.

If the factor is valid, then the purpose and conduct of life, and the inevitable death, must be related to it. Otherwise the whole phenomenon and performance of existence is ultimately meaningless.

*

In the English language, the original and ultimate causal factor has commonly come to be called "God".

Translated from the Arabic, the sound of the name of the factor is represented in the hieroglyphs we are using in this book by the letters "Allah".

Other religions use other sounds and other hieroglyphs.

Whichever sound we use—and there are many of them in the languages of the world—it will not matter for our purposes. The difference between one religion and another only consists in how, from time to time and from place to place, different people have believed, and how they now believe, it is valid to comprehend and relate to the Absolute Factor, and how to express that comprehension and relationship.

As suggested above, the crucial difficulty arises from the concept of "oneness" itself and how to keep it pure.

For example, having proposed God as the whole, the one totality, that which caused the universe, there is an immediate paradox: God *and* the universe. Two? If God is the totality, how can there be a separate universe as well? And what about me? God *and* the universe and *me*? Three?

Who conceived the apparent division between God and the universe?

I did. It is me who is holding the concept of them being separate.

What, then, happens if the concept of me being separate dissolves?

Who then is there to think God separate from the universe?

And did I not conceive that God is the Absolute Factor, the One that must, by definition, be everything?

Therefore, cannot the only possible solution to the riddle be that I should understand that I am not individual and separate?

Where then would be my aloneness, incompleteness and ignorance?

How can there possibly be God *and* me?

One of us is an illusion!

Who, then, am I?

*

The above is one rather simple—and some might say primitive—approach to what has come to be called "religion".

It would seem to suggest that Man proposed or invented God.

The atheist might well claim that that is what Man did and does, and that it is absurd, having proposed the unprovable, then to proceed to believe in it.

But . . . a strange, mystical element enters if we pursue a little further.

Yes, it could be said that Man invented God . . . *but what caused him to do it?*

Why did and does he do it?

Would Man do such a thing wilfully and pointlessly?

What is going on?

*

What causes Man's intelligence to conceive of the Absolute Factor and then to attempt to comprehend It, relate to It, aspire to It?

Could it be that the Absolute Factor causes human intelligence to work in a certain way in order to accomplish something in relation to Itself?

Could it be that in his religious concern Man is working in direct relationship with the Absolute Factor . . . regardless of how he may explain it to himself from time to time?

If it is a delusion of his mind to think himself separate, would not the resolution of the problem lie in the dispersal of that delusion?

It could be that the Absolute Factor accomplishes "something" through the mind of Man . . . whether that mind comprehends it or not?

*

He is close to us, but we are far from him. The place where he dwells is inaccessible, and no tongue is able to utter his name. Before him hang a hundred thousand veils of light and darkness, and in the two worlds no one has power to dispute his kingdom. He is the sovran lord and is bathed in the perfection of his majesty. He does not manifest himself completely even in the place of his dwelling, and to this no knowledge or intelligence can attain. The way is unknown, and no one has the steadfastness to seek it, though thousands of creatures spend their lives in longing. Even the purest soul cannot describe him, neither can the reason comprehend: these two eyes are blind. The wise cannot discover his perfection nor can the man of understanding perceive his beauty. All creatures have wished to attain to this perfection and beauty by imagination. But how can you tread that path with thought? How measure the moon from the fish?

(*The Conference of the Birds*)

III

So, then, the knower and that which he knows are both one, and he who unites and that with which he unites are one, and seer and seen are one. For the knower is His attribute and the known is His essence; and he who unites is His attribute, and that with which he unites is His essence; and the attribute and that to which it is attributed are one. And this is the explanation of the saying "Whoso knoweth himself knoweth his Lord."

(*Ibn 'Arabi*)

*

Having himself thought "god", why does Man worry as to whether there is a god or not?

How can he hope to comprehend and relate with certainty to something he has himself imagined?

Immediately the mind projects the idea "god", there is the possibility of fall into the separation "me *and* god".

This is a curious paradox!

Unless and until I question who it is who is thinking "I am."

Rather than pursuing the god "out there", would it not be more appropriate to enquire who is doing the pursuing?

*

Man proposes the Absolute or Causal Factor and calls it by many names, including "God".

He then attempts to comprehend the nature of that Factor and according to what certain men assert to be the essence and attributes of that nature, so other men are moved and persuaded

13

to behave and believe in accordance with that assertion and its implications.

Those who have been most effective in their proclamations (in certain traditions called "prophets") have, for one reason or another over the passing centuries, captured the attention and inspired thousands, even millions, of followers. The legacy of their influence is manifest in the notable religions and philosophies which we find in the world today.

How can we account for the enormous influence of those men and their teaching?

Not easy!

One proposition we could make is this: that given a certain power or faculty of mind, either by "accident" of birth or applied self-development, or both, they were able to comprehend and relate to the Absolute Factor. Such was the "depth" or "height" of this understanding that they were able to express their knowledge of it with utter conviction. We could say that to a degree greater than those around them, they were closer to the viewpoint of the Ultimate; or conversely, they had to a greater degree surrendered themselves to the reality of the Absolute Factor. Perhaps they had been able to do so completely, in which case nothing remained of self-will or self-identity in them. Such was the completeness of their understanding, they were able to convey in their own words the resolution of the mystical questions. We can imagine that in the presence of such power, those seeking alleviation from aloneness, incompleteness and ignorance could well be attracted. Such would be the powerful magnetism of the religious leader.

Of course, "lesser", temporal leaders have comparative power and influence due to their conviction in mundane affairs. They attract their followers because of their ability to persuade that, given the power, they can provide security. But we are concerned here only with the highest, supramundane aspirations experienced by the human mind. None of the religious leaders worthy of consideration were interested in worldly power. Their contention has always been that if men exercise their minds to comprehend and relate to the Absolute Factor, and see the world and its affairs from that perspective, then mundane concerns can be properly evaluated and become relatively insignificant.

Different religious leaders have used different methods of expression and have placed emphasis on different emotions in order to stimulate their audiences. And the record of their utterances suggest that they spoke in the character of their time and place and according to the level and character of particular audiences.

In this book we will be considering the expression of religion called Islam which derives from the life, example, experiences and utterances of a man named Muhammad (or Mohammed), born twelve centuries ago, claimed by his followers to be "The Prophet". His sacred message is recorded in the book called the Qur'an (or Koran).

*

Will the message of Islam enable us to answer our profoundest questions?

That will depend on whether its mode of expression finds response in our own experience . . . and whether we are moved to enquire deeply and with perseverance. The latter is *really* the governing factor.

The questions are the spur . . . the thorns which prick our cocoon of pre-occupation, self-concern and complacency.

Do the questions haunt and nag throughout the experience we call life?

Not all the time; not always with the same intensity; not at the beginning.

But they *are* there, now, aren't they?

Are we afraid of them?

The enquiry begins when we realize that they are vitally important, and not just idle dreams or speculations.

What is it that we are really looking for, even in all our daily concerns and activity?

Why, as human beings, should we be looking for anything?

15

Even if we are fortunate to have friends and loved ones, even if we have all the material needs and pleasures we could hope for, even if we have had years of education and the world's wisdom is at our disposal . . . why is there still this sense of being alone, of lacking lasting satisfaction and fulfilment, of not knowing what is really important about life itself? It is almost as if the world's idea of being mature and adult is some game of make-believe; underneath there is still the same innocent and vulnerable child . . . waiting to be shown the reality. To this child inside, what the world takes so seriously seems like some lunatic and absurd façade.

*

A Sufi woke one night and said to himself: It seems to me that the world is like a chest in which we are put and the lid shut down, and we give ourselves up to foolishness. When death lifts the lid, he who has acquired wings, soars away to eternity, but he who has not, stays in the chest a prey to a thousand tribulations. Make sure then that the bird of ambition acquires wings of aspiration, and give to your heart and reason the ecstasy of the soul. Before the lid of the chest is opened become a bird of the Spirit, ready to spread your wings.

(*A Sufi story*)

*

If we care to study the evolution of different schools of concept, thought, belief and self-discipline over the millennia of recorded history, we will find examples of great debate and conviction giving direction and inspiration to thousands. Such discipline of emotion provides extraordinary examples of courage and sacrifice—and has also on occasions resulted in the slaughter of thousands.

How will it avail us to adopt one school of thought as opposed to another; one religious tradition as opposed to another?

How can we decide intellectually the over-riding merits of one form of belief to the exclusion of all others?

Patterns of words and sounds; that is the medium through which we are informed of man's experience and which we have to interpret.

How can they communicate to us about the most noble and worth-while pursuit of all—the quest for truth concerning our earthly existence?

Surely we cannot do it just by thinking about it and debating it in abstract?

In a matter so personally crucial as the purpose and fulfilment of our own lives here and now, surely we have to call upon every human faculty, every facet of our being, every item of experience?

There is a tendency to compartmentalize our lives. There are what we call ordinary, everyday activities—because they are common to all men in general. And there are specialized activities such as religious practice and philosophical study, which we tend to think of as only pursued by minorities.

This is surely an artificial and absurd differentiation?

In the broadest of terms and deepest of meaning, *how* I do any-thing—in the home, the office, the street, the factory, anywhere—is based on "my philosophy" as to how things should be done. However commonplace and makeshift, this philosophy of life is derived from my particular learning and experience. And *what* I decide to do, however commonplace, is based on "my religion". This again is derived from my experience of what pleases me and interests me and hence what I choose to devote my time and energies to—broadly speaking, what I believe in and worship.

The real question therefore is not whether I am religious or philosophical but whether my religion and philosophy is effective and fulfilling.

If I think or feel that my life is lacking, then I may begin to consider other men's religions and philosophies to see if they can help me to improve mine.

The point about this is that there is no such thing in itself as *a* religion or *a* philosophy, as if such things existed in themselves, clear-cut and self-explanatory. The only reality in either religion or philosophy is what I make of it; and in this sense it inevitably becomes "my" religion and "my" philosophy.

Therefore in looking at the religions and philosophies of the world—that is to say, the recorded bits and pieces of other men's religions and philosophies—we will never find *the* religion or *the* philosophy. There is no such thing, "out there". It is quite simply that what information we can gather may help us modify and improve *our own* religions and philosophies.

It is a bit like, say, an apple on a tree. It is very beautiful hanging there. Certainly I admire it. I can touch it and I can smell it. I might even write a poem about it and sing a ballad about it. I could claim that it is the most beautiful and perfect apple there has ever been. But what is the purpose of it? Some would say its purpose is to fill us with joy; it is a "gift from God". That's fair enough providing I am not hungry at that moment. Is its purpose to produce seeds to grow several more apple trees? Is the purpose of the tree to cover the surface of the earth in its own likeness? The fact is that if I look at it long enough I become hungry and eat it. The apple becomes me.

*

The attempt by man to comprehend and relate to the Absolute Factor—rather than settle for a mundane, precarious and wilful existence—may be regarded as his worthiest aspiration. It is this aspiration which has given rise to what we have named "religion" and "philosophy".

Whether or not you and I wish to participate in it appears to be our individual choice.

But what moves us? What awakens the aspiration in us?

If I contemplate my present existence, what is the answer if I ask myself, "Is there really a quest for me?"

*

But you must know God by Himself and not by you; it is He who opens the way that leads to Him, not human wisdom . . .

*

Is there a quest for me—really?

This, the first question on the way, is the most difficult one.

Any question can only be effective NOW. It is useless saying that yesterday these was a quest for me or tomorrow I may be searching again.

Immediate . . . NOW . . . is there a quest for me, really?

*

There are two reasons for making a journey.

The first is that you are not content with where you are and just wish to be somewhere else.

The second is that there is a place you have heard of that you want to go to . . . and it sounds attractive.

Often these two reasons come hand in hand. In other words, you are not content with where you are and you have heard about another place that would be, you imagine, preferable.

So you leave the first place and attempt to reach the second place.

On the other hand, if you are fully content where you are then the other place can have nothing better to offer you and you will not wish to move.

*

Only a fool—or a wise man—would give up contentment and fulfilment and make a journey into the unknown.

A fool will do so "wilfully". Lacking any judgement, in the world's terms, he will make the journey simply because it offers him the unknown . . . and, who can say, perhaps even greater contentment at the end?

A wise man will make the journey because of his judgement and discernment, welcoming the challenge to know the unknown as a way of discovering what the contentment was that he experienced before he set off.

*

The daring of the fools of God is a good thing. They cannot tell if the way is good or bad, they only know how to act.

(*A Sufi saying*)

*

Am I foolish or wise?

The world, in its own terms, may judge me either. In its terms, I may also consider myself foolish or wise, from time to time, in relation to my actions.

But if I disregard the world's terms, who is to say whether in any real terms I am one or the other?

I may be both or neither.

But will I make the journey?

If I am to make the journey, it will not be because my life "here" is unbearable. I am persuaded—worldly advantages and disadvantages apart—that it is neither better nor worse than the life common to all men. I am subject to the same dualities. I have some advantages and some disadvantages; sometimes I am happy, sometimes sad; sometimes I am "up", sometimes "down". I do not question why this should be so. Why am I influenced this way and that by what happens to me? Why should I be happy sometimes and sometimes not? Perhaps that is how it has to be? Perhaps there is no alternative? No "escape"? Unless I undertake the journey, how can I know?

*

An idiot of God went naked and starving along the road in winter. With neither house nor shelter he was soaked with rain and sleet. At last he came to a ruined palace and decided to take refuge there, but as he went in through the doorway a tile fell on his head and cracked his skull, so that the blood flowed. He turned his face to heaven and said: "Wouldn't it be better to beat the royal drum than to drop a tile on my head?"

(*A Sufi story*)

*

Who makes the journey?

If I think that I do, when I am there it will be here—and what was here will be there.

20

The art of making the journey is that I leave myself, wise or foolish, behind . . . "the flight of the unknown to the unknown".

*

Today, the world is well trodden. There is hardly "anywhere" left to discover; eventually there will be "nowhere" left.

And so Man has turned his attention to that which lies beyond this world.

We have built rockets and sent men to the moon. Now our sights are set further afield—to the planets and the stars and the far galaxies.

What do we hope to find there?

Whatever the purpose, one of the most significant aspects of the first journey to the moon was that men were able to look back at the whole globe of earth—"the good earth" as one of them called it. By leaving their home, they were able to look back at it, to stand apart from it, for the first time.

By making my journey, perhaps I will see myself, objectively, for the first time.

Know thyself.

To know myself, I must see myself.

To see myself, I must stand apart from me and look . . . from the unknown.

Only from the unknown can there be knowing.

To step outside myself is to enter the unknown—just as to step outside the earth's atmosphere is to enter "space".

*

Is there a quest for me—really?

If there is a quest—there is The Quest.

I cannot deny it—simply because, for *me*, it is there.

If there is no quest for you—there is no Quest.

You cannot deny nor ignore it—simply because, for *you*, it does not exist.

How can you ignore that which does not exist? It isn't possible.

If it exists for you, then it is undeniable—and irresistible—simply because, if it exists for you, *you are already on it*.

It is not something that you either join or don't join through choice. It either *is*—or it isn't.

As such it is an entirely individual experience.

If it is there, you are on it!

If you are not on it—there isn't an "it" to be on!

*

. . . But Allah leaves in error whom He will and guides whom He pleases . . .

(*The Qur'an, Surah 14*)

*

A series of conundrums? Perhaps.

But that is the nature of the approach to the Absolute Factor and the nature of the comprehending and relating to it.

It is the essence of the mystery of the relationship between God and Man.

Intellect operates in the known. It cannot function in the unknown; it simply eliminates itself. At first it is useful in demonstrating the relative. It is rather like the first stage of the space rocket; it takes the traveller to the edge of the known, provides the velocity necessary to counteract the gravity of earth; then it is discarded as being of no further use for the flight.

So it is as we enter "space".

Or rather, that is how we describe it.

To "enter" it suggests that we were not hitherto in it.

How can that be?

Out in the space of mind, the orbiting thoughts, the frameworks of belief and the known dimensions of fact cease to be relevant. The laws that apply to "earth", "water", "fire" and "air" cease to operate.

It is a further dimension, where time does not exist.

Are we then "there" already?

Who goes "to the stars"?

22

Are the stars "out there"—millions of light years away from us—or are they images in my mind?

Consider . . . (from two Latin words meaning "with the stars").

What is "SPACE"?

*

He is close to us, but we are far from him. The place where he dwells is inaccessible, and no tongue is able to utter his name.

IV

So, let me consider . . .
admitting that there is a quest for me . . .
what am I looking for?

*

A hundred different things on a hundred different occasions.
Sometimes I might express it as needing love; sometimes understanding; sometimes knowledge or wisdom; sometimes peace;
sometimes excitement, entertainment, pleasure . . . Any of these
might express my inner aloneness, incompleteness or ignorance,
from time to time.

Surely there is a universality in this search?

But it is *me* who feels it. I would say that I need someone to love
me, understand *me*, and it is *me* who wants the peace and the
excitement.

It is a pretty exhausting pursuit.

So why do I continue?

Because sometimes I appear to succeed. With luck, I find those
who say they love me, those who say they understand me, those who
will provide knowledge and wisdom. Sometimes I find the peace,
the excitement, the entertainment, the pleasure . . .

The trouble is, the good fortune is either short-lived or precarious . . . at least difficult to maintain.

And I am also just as likely to run into dislike, misunderstanding,
frustration, turmoil and pain.

So what am I *really* looking for?

The permanent in the ocean of impermanence? The everlasting

experience in a transient world? The changeless Truth in a fog of fashionable opinion?

A love that lasts for ever?

A complete understanding?

A knowledge that outlives all passing knowing, that encompasses every aspect of my experience from birth through to inevitable death?

Could I ever find such things on earth?

*

We appear to have only one choice when we have explored all the options open to us.

We simply accept our fate. We accept the limits of our comprehension and live a life within the world's laws, relying on man's definitions and explanations, striving to maintain as comfortable and enjoyable a life as possible, hoping for our share of love, understanding, peace, pleasure and excitement. To help us, we sometimes allow the god-idea; it may provide a focus for our expression of gratitude for the blessings and the good times; and an alleviation for the tension and disturbance when things go wrong; and it will provide an easy account for the inexplicable.

Thus, we will traverse a limited period of historical time—"my life"—ignorant of our beginning and apprehensive of our end.

Or, alternatively, through observation and experience, we can refuse to accept that that is all there is to it. In no way does that situation answer my deepest questions nor satisfy what I am really looking for. Once we have admitted the limitation and precariousness of our conditioned learning and belief, and are prepared to forsake it, then we truly reach the point where we are on the threshold of the unknown.

What then?

Step into it.

What does that mean?

It means surrender or submission.

Of what?

The "me" that is born of self-will . . . and all my beliefs and opinions which create my idea of the world.

Difficult?

The "me" is going to die anyway, eventually. Why not give it up now and see what happens?

Of course, it may not happen overnight! It may take years and years. Neither is it easy—as we may gather from the account of others who have undertaken it.

Rather like the fledgling bird flexing his wings on the edge of the nest, we may be reluctant to take the first step. We may approach the threshold over and over again and then retreat to the familiar. But sooner or later, the launch into space will take place; in the end, we have to die to ourselves.

*

What happens if we dare to transcend earth-bound definitions?

Do we not have hints?

When we give ourselves up to the love of someone, where then the aloneness, the incompleteness, the ignorance?

Are we then not prepared to be consumed, to surrender all? And are we not willing to surrender ourselves every night to the peace of sleep?

*

O lovers, O lovers, it is time to abandon the world:

The drum of departure reaches my spiritual ear from heaven.

Behold, the driver has risen and made ready his files of camels,

And begged us to acquit him of blame: why, O travellers, are you asleep?

These sounds before and behind are the din of departure and of the camel-bells;

With each moment a soul and spirit is setting off into the Void.

From these inverted candles, from these blue awnings,

There has come forth a wondrous people, that the mysteries may be revealed.

A heavy slumber fell upon thee from the circling spheres:
Alas, for this life so light, beware of this slumber so heavy!
O soul, seek the Beloved, O friend, seek the Friend,
O watchman, be wakeful: it behoves not a watchman to sleep.

(*The Journey to the Beloved*, Jalalu'd-din Rumi)

*

We have spoken of the quest for truth in the world's terms. Now we are speaking of The Quest—the flight of the unknown to the unknown—when all self-will has been abandoned, when all beliefs have melted away and there is nought left but "faith".

For the purposes of this book, it is at this level and in this context that we propose to speak of "the believer" and "the unbeliever" as terms repeated so frequently in the theme of the Qur'an.

The believer is simply one who has surrendered self-will and has faith.

The unbeliever is simply one who through self-will puts his faith in any self-conceptualized image.

Thus it is in a transcendental sense that we consider the Absolute Factor, Allah.

The believer who has surrendered self-will to the Will of Allah merges into the Absolute Factor, the Totality.

The unbeliever through his own will worships "something"—which he may even call Allah. The point is that in doing so he still reserves his own separateness. For him, it is still "me and Allah whom I worship". He has still not totally surrendered.

This short-fall from total surrender to the Absolute Factor is the kind of misconception which splinters "true religiousness" into a thousand conflicting forms of religion. Because men conceive their gods we apparently have different religions and we learn of Allah, God, Jehovah, Brahman and so on as if they were competing champions. Religiousness has nothing to do with "your god" and "my god". They are all just names for the Absolute Factor. Religiousness ("the binding back" to unity) is concerned with re-union of the apparently separate with the One and Only Ultimate Principle. In so many words, this is what Muhammad emphasized over and over again.

*

Thus, if someone asks you "Do you believe there is a god?" how can you possibly answer?

All you can reasonably say is something like: "If you will tell me what you mean by a god, then perhaps I will be able to tell you whether I believe there is one or not."

Likewise, someone may ask you "Do you believe in God (or Allah, or Brahman, or whatever)?"

Again, the answer must depend, if there is to be one, on some mutually agreed definition of the term "in God".

And what definition can there possibly be?

Any definition or conception as to the essence or attributes of the Absolute Factor immediately draws the discussion into the realms of relative belief and opinion—man-envisaged at that.

The question, if it is to have any real worth, can only be directed at oneself:

Do I believe in God?

Then I must search my own mind to understand what I mean by the question.

Ideally, by a process of eliminating what I do not mean by it, I may understand.

. . . But you must know God by Himself and not by you . . .

*

If you ask me whether I believe in God, I can tell you whether I do or don't. But what is that to you . . . if I cannot possibly *tell you* what I experience and mean by it?

When at first I am introduced to the god-idea I struggle to comprehend such an idea. It is not at all easy, even though my "tutors", whoever they may be, seem to have faith in this god as if it were some established fact of life.

28

But I cannot relate what they seem to be saying to my own experience. For the time being, I have to take their word for it and perhaps acknowledge that the idea is a possible resolution of the problem as to who caused or created everything and perhaps even a way of coping with all the inexplicable mysteries of existence. I may perhaps even privately nurture some image or concept of this anthropomorphic Almighty Being.

But it is all rather vague and unsubstantial.

It will be a considerable step for me to be so convinced—or self-persuaded—that I can myself assert to others that "I believe in God."

And it is a considerable step from there to accepting in due course that I have invented the whole concept and have got it all the wrong way round.

*

One of the curious features of theological debate is that it all seems to concentrate on establishing as fact the existence, nature and attributes of the supreme deity: "How can God be proved?" "How can God be comprehended?" "How should we worship God?" and so on. All this results in theory after theory, one school of persuasion after another. Such is the concentration on the supposed object, "God", that seemingly no one seems to query what the capacity and act of "believing" *is* as man experiences it. And, above all, the subject, the "I" is entirely overlooked. Who *is* the "I" who is doing the believing?

The act of believing is something we can observe in our own experience. It is important that we should do just that—because it has enormous consequence on the conduct of our lives.

One way of describing it is that it is a mental process whereby the subject, "I", gives or leases itself, its life, its being, to the establishment of something. I commit myself to my own interpretation of my own concept of what something means to me.

It is not easy to describe but if I really do observe what my believing is I will see that I am investing my life in "something".

This is an extremely serious thing to do, for, once I have done it, inevitably that belief will rule me for as long as it is held.

In my early years I am led into belief very easily, for I have very limited experience and my powers of discrimination and evaluation are either undeveloped or powerless. It is quite possible for the beliefs to become so embodied and established that when the power of discrimination does develop it begins to operate *on the basis* of those beliefs. It may be some time (perhaps never) before it actually questions *the validity of the beliefs themselves.*

The trouble is that we become fearful of such questioning. Why? Because we think we depend on the beliefs. They seem to be the basis of our security. Above all, I will hang on to the belief that I know who I am. "I am me!"

*

Thus, assuming I know who I am, I am confronted with the problem as to whether I can believe in the existence of God or not. What extraordinary audacity to think that God depends on whether I choose to believe in him or not!

What kind of madness is it that persuades man that he can choose whether there is a "God" or not when he does not even know who or what he is himself!

Nevertheless, this is the situation I find myself in.

I totally disregard what "believing" is and ignore who "I" am— the one who is doing the believing.

I assume I know who I am—me, this person here—and everyone knows what believing is, and therefore the only problem is who "God" is.

*

The key principle, emphasized over and over again by Muhammad, is stated, for example, in Surah 112 of the Qur'an:

. . . *Allah is One, the Eternal God. He begot none, nor was He begotten. None is equal to Him.*

*

30

How then do "I" fit in?

Me *and* God?

Can there be both of us?

Allah is One . . .

If Allah is One . . . who is me? . . . and you? . . . and everyone else?

Certainly there is a body sitting here. Certainly it has a name. There is a mind that thinks that this is me . . . the person going about in the world. But who am I . . . the one observing all this?

If the mind is truly honest (empty, and therefore not deceived), it does not know who the "I" is—the *centre* of this particular being and experience—and it does not know who "God" is—the One Totality, the all-containing *circumference*.

*

The questions keep bubbling up in my mind:

What is going on in this experience I call "mind"?

If this person "me" is caused and created by "God", and then this person "me" comes to believe in this "God", and then this person "me" dies . . . what has happened?

Who is doing what to whom?

What can the mind understand and have faith *in* with absolute certainty?

*

And then there is this alternative:

I, whoever I am, appear to have the possibility, given the will and the power, of ignoring, suppressing, eliminating "me". I can consciously act without self-concern and self-will. I can act without desire for myself.

In that situation, whose will operates?

*

My will or "The Will of Allah"?

There is only the Will of Allah . . . even my will is the Will of Allah.

*

. . . *the fools of God . . . cannot tell if the way is good or bad, they only know how to act.*

V

We, the authors of this book, are not Arabs; nor were we brought up in an Arab environment; we do not speak nor read Arabic; nor have we been taught and become accustomed to Muslim practices.

We are therefore not familiar with the sounds of Islam nor their effects on the mind.

All these experiences would, of course, be crucial to understanding and being able to speak authentically about the emotion and feeling of "being Muslim".

The continual repetition of ritual and disciplines, and the recitation day after day of sacred words, plays an important role in providing strength and comfort in any religion. We cannot therefore hope to convey, for example, what long-term effect the experience of reciting and listening to the Qur'an has on one who is grounded in that practice.

All we have for the purposes of considering the nature of Islam, as far as the sacred scriptural basis of it is concerned, is someone's attempt to translate the meaning of the Arabic into contemporary English.

What can we hope to do in one short book with such apparent limitation?

We can only consider what illumination or confirmation those translated scriptures can provide for us, here and now.

*

In conjunction with the historical record of the reported life of Muhammad himself, we can regard the majority of what is said in

33

the Qur'an at the literal level as being appropriate to the time, the place and the society in which it originated. Unless we are interested in the religion in order to learn about its historical origins, its development, its practices and its outward presentation, then all the instruction about moral, social and legal conduct, and so forth, will not in itself help us to understand the strength and character of Islam as a *religious* movement. These "nuts and bolts" certainly do not account for the spread of what has become a major world religion; nor do they account for the apparently extraordinary fact that one man was able to "start another religion" in an area which was already well endowed with several different religions and schools of thought.

Furthermore, the particular benefits gained by the millions who have followed that instruction over the centuries is also not likely to be relevant to our quest for the meaning of "religiousness" itself—unless we are convinced that there is exclusive religious benefit to be derived from "being Muslim" in particular.

If you do happen to think so, then the enquiry of this book may not be for you, for, as we have suggested on several occasions in this series, religiousness is a human state of mind which transcends all the forms of religion which attempt to express it.

*

So, how can the Islamic scriptures help us?

They may throw a shaft of light from another angle—related to, but not exactly the same as, other traditions.

We are looking for a glimpse of any light that Islam can shed on the mystery of our own experience—regardless of whether, for the time being, we happen to call ourselves Muslims, Buddhists, Jews, Hindus, Christians, atheists or whatever.

*

We have already selected one key principle, the one which forms the basis for the whole Muslim faith (as, in other words, it is the fundamental basis of all other monotheistic religions):

. . . Allah is One, the Eternal God. He begets none, nor was He begotten. None is equal to Him.

Why should this one principle have such enormous implication?

Because it states explicitly how the Absolute Factor should be conceived of in the human mind.

All the rest hangs upon this one statement.

And according to comprehension of its implications, so will there be understanding in the mind . . . in my mind, in your mind, in anyone's mind . . . regardless of any particular form of religion.

That is to say, understanding ("standing under") in its most pure and religious sense—that of surrender or submission—the meaning of the word "Islam".

*

Theologically speaking, there was nothing new in Muhammad's essential and forceful message. It had been stated in other words back through the centuries before his time by the Jews and Christians especially. He simply re-affirmed it in his own language.

But let us consider a little the background to Muhammad's testament to see why he emerged as "The Prophet".

He was born in Mecca (about half-way down the eastern side of the Red Sea in Saudi Arabia) about fourteen centuries ago and although he was born about five and a half centuries after the reported death of Jesus, he was as distant from Moses in history as we are distant from Jesus. In other words, Moses is said to have lived about three and a half thousand years ago, Jesus two thousand years ago, and Muhammad between thirteen and fourteen hundred years ago.

These are perhaps interesting facts and figures. In a curious way, because we can count the years and place events in a logical, historical sequence, then there seems to be a reassuring continuity, as though we are in some tangible way related to them. In experience this is extremely tenuous and may be very deceptive.

It is actually impossible to *experience* duration of time. We can remember events that happened an hour ago, yesterday, last year, maybe many years ago. We can place the events of our lives in sequence. We can usually remember the image of the event and we can possibly say we remember how joyful, beautiful, depressing, frightening it was. But we cannot actually *re-experience* it. It is only, as it were, "fictionally" related to us, as we are here and now, in the present. Thus we can only very vaguely project ourselves back into the past of our lives. We can relate what happened to us but we cannot re-live it. We can relate many things that happened yesterday, several that happened last month, a few that happened last year, single significant events over the last decade, and then . . . And this is our own life we are considering . . . that which we have ourselves experienced. So what kind of worth and validity is there to us in events that happened to other people thousands and thousands of years ago? Not only do we not have the element of personal experience but we cannot possibly comprehend such spans of time.

Leading on from that, and applying it to this particular enquiry, we can be misled in another way. In this present life we can observe, and perhaps experience, modern Islam, modern Judaism and modern Christianity as co-existent. Apart from the fact that we may tend to think that basically each one has always been the same and that, say, "being a Muslim" today is the same as "being a Muslim" was five hundred years ago, we cannot comprehend what it would be like to live in a Judaic society where there was as yet no such thing as a Christian or a Muslim, or, later, to live in a Judaic and Christian society where there was as yet no such thing as a Muslim. We cannot comprehend the hundreds and thousands of years that separated their inception; and we can no more imagine with validity the experience of being in the time and place of Muhammad himself than we could imagine, say, the state of religion a thousand years hence.

The so-called "facts" about Muhammad then are some bits and pieces of information recorded well over a thousand years ago; the "fiction" is what I make of those facts—how I fashion them. The paradox is, *in my experience now*, that it is the "facts" that seem unreal and that it is my fashioning of them, the "fiction", that seems real . . . has relevance.

*

Muhammad's father died about the time Muhammad was born and his mother died whilst he was still a child. He was brought up first by his grandfather and then by an uncle, apparently beneficially for he became well respected for his good sense and integrity.

As a young man he travelled with the trading caravans to Syria and evidently became well acquainted with the religious beliefs and practices of the region—Jewish and Christian sects and various pagan cults. ("Pagan" tends to have been used by Jews and Christians to signify those who didn't happen to share their forms of belief.)

It seems that Muhammad was drawn to the concept of monotheism and was particularly influenced by a group called the *hanif*, who lived austere lives as ascetics and who rejected all forms of idolatry. We can surmise that it was from this discipline of thought that the later evolution of Muhammad's message emerged.

It must have been in obedience to their disciplines and practices that, somewhere around the age of forty, Muhammad retired for a period alone to a cave in Mount Hira for prayer, contemplation, meditation . . . or whatever they happened to call it at the time. One night—whilst asleep, or in a trance, or, say, whilst the mind was void of thinking—"he heard a voice" (which he later decided was the voice of the angel Gabriel) urging him, "Recite!"

It is said that he was at first confused as to what it was intended he should recite and was, in any case, reluctant to do so because he thought he might be suffering from some kind of hallucination or going mad. But "the angel" persisted and eventually he assented and began "to speak".

*

What can we make of this—how can we fashion it—to satisfy our

37

twentieth-century minds (or, say, fourteenth-century minds, in Islamic terms)?

In this scientific age we are unlikely to think in terms of angels visiting us. But, in those moments when our minds are void of deliberate thinking, we might, for example, pause to wonder why we have dreamed what we have dreamed or to wonder where a certain idea that "drops into the mind" has come from.

How would we explain such things?

Each according to his learning and observation of experience. We might explain the dreams away in the terms of modern psychology. Desires and fears playing havoc with an illogical mixture of memory impressed images. And as far as the inspirational idea is concerned . . . well, how do you explain where that came from?

If I suddenly think of something, entirely unexpected, not worked out, coming "out of the blue", can I honestly say that I originated it? I may well claim that I thought it but, really, where did it come from? If it is really so inexplicable, I might just as well say an angel spoke to me as anything else.

And what do I do when I have had a good idea?

It is usually irresistible and I go ahead and express it.

It may result in my taking certain actions on my own account. On the other hand if it is an idea I think worth sharing, I will be prompted (by whom or what? The same angel?) to tell someone, to relate it, to "recite" (to "set moving . . . again").

But supposing it is some revolutionary idea? Supposing that it prompts me to do or say something that is quite outside my habitual mode of conduct, that it is not likely to be at all popular or that it requires me to act as I have never acted before? For a start, I am likely at least to be reluctant!

And supposing what I suddenly realize revolutionises what I have always thought? Supposing it shatters what I have always believed? Supposing it reveals and suggests to me that I have been deluded, that what I have trusted was a total illusion, that my life has been a pursuit in the wrong direction, that what I have thought worth doing has been a complete waste of time? Would I readily trust such a revelation? Would I not wonder if I was somehow the victim of a hallucination, that I was going mad?

Ideas of that calibre have a habit of persisting! They do not just go away; they keep coming back, again and again.

And so, I may well obey . . . and act and speak.

In ignorance, I may well claim that it was *my* idea . . . and may perhaps claim the reward or suffer the consequences.

But if I am objective, I know that the idea was not "mine" and that in my acting and speaking in response to the idea, it is as though the idea, or whatever it is, is working *through* me, using me as its vehicle of expression.

I do not know what (or who) is working through me . . . fourteen centuries ago I might have thought it was "Allah". And I may well have expressed the experience of my part in the propagation of it as being rather like "a messenger".

There is nothing unique in all this. We may be in awe or be sceptical of an apparently magical or mystical experience, something that used to happen to people in ages gone by. On the other hand, my having ideas is comparatively ordinary. But is it really? Is not the occurrence of an inspirational idea a magical and mystical experience . . . if we really stop to consider it?

What is the difference between the two . . . other than the terms in which it is expressed and the degree of significance?

Certainly I have lots of ideas which are trivial and lots that come to nothing. But here we come to another factor.

An idea is only effective in the degree to which it meets a suitable deployment of circumstances in which to operate. The most marvellous idea is useless if it cannot find response—rather like a seed of great potential which simply rots if it cannot take root in suitable earth.

The potential of an idea is only realized if it arises in the right time, the right place and the right circumstances. It would be pointless my originating the Qur'an *now*. If I said Allah was speaking through me via the angel Gabriel I would probably be gently steered to somewhere where I wouldn't be a nuisance to other people.

But what Muhammad realized in that cave at that time was highly relevant to the state of religion then . . . as indeed, in other terms, it is *now*.

VI

What could we suggest Muhammad realized when, alone in the cave of Mount Hira, he became inspired?

What was the essence of the message and why was it so powerful and provocative that men should have been prepared to fight and die for it at that time and over the succeeding centuries and, coincidentally, be the platform for a world religion with millions upon millions of followers?

*

Undoubtedly Muhammad realized the nature of man's relationship with the Absolute Factor and what steps were necessary for any man to comprehend it. In his terms, he understood the Will of Allah. And in his comprehension of the relationship, he saw that the established religions of the world had fallen short in their understanding and had compromised with the full implications of that relationship. This is not to suggest that he alone was truly religious—far from it. It was simply that the formalized performance of contemporary religion had gone astray and the official representations of those religions were propagating doctrines, beliefs and practices which were not *truly* religious.

Thus, it was not a case of him being suddenly inspired to "start a new religion". Rather it was a case, having realized how formal religion had compromised itself, of having the courage to proclaim and re-affirm the eternal and uncompromisable Truth of the One God. Perhaps we can appreciate his initial reluctance to speak out. He would by implication be bound to be seeming to denounce the contemporary establishment, regardless of whether there happened

41

to be truly religious Jews and Christians in it or not. And certainly those who considered themselves to have exclusive access to theological truth, and saw their power, authority and security on earth to be dependent on maintaining that exclusivity, did react violently.

*

In the Qur'an we find that Muhammad had no quarrel with the original Jewish and Christian teachings. He affirmed that many of the Jewish prophets—notably Noah, Abraham, Moses and David—were true proclaimers (that is to say, men who understood and truly "revealed God's Will", or in our terminology, men who had uncompromisingly aligned themselves with the Absolute Factor). He also affirmed that Jesus of Nazareth had been a true prophet of the One God. But, over the millennia since Moses and the centuries since Jesus, the Jews and the Christians had distorted the original teachings, misinterpreted them, fallen into ignorant and degenerating schisms, upheld divisive dogma as truth, corrupted pure faith, established themselves in temporal hierarchies and positions which had created false barriers between the people and the Truth of the One God, deviated from obedience to natural law, exercised their will in adopting heretical and absurd prejudices, and so on.

Above all, and implicit in all these observations, Muhammad saw that true religiousness had degenerated into idolatry. And we should consider by this that not only had the officials of established religion and its followers strayed into idolization at a material level—worshipping images, representations, worldly attributes and possessions, and so on—but had also adopted and worshipped false and deluding concepts, beliefs and myths. For example, the Christians idolized the man Jesus and, having endowed him with attributes and powers which he himself had been at pains to disclaim in his own lifetime, now made claims as to his special relationship with the One God, even believing that he was some kind of semi-divine human being, the one and only example of

God's intervention in the affairs of the world. Muhammad saw such self-deceptive make-believe as totally antipathetic to the equality and freedom of all men in their religious comprehension and relationship with the Absolute Factor, which he called Allah for want of a name. "By all means," he might have said, "acknowledge the man Jesus as one who so under-stood the Will of Allah that he might be termed one who truly spoke and acted in obedience to 'it'—as a son may obey his father—and, by all means seek to understand what he said and attempt to emulate his example, but do not worship him and set him up as an idol."

For the crucial principle, as Muhammad expressed it, was that "Allah is One, the Eternal God. He begot none, nor was He begotten. None is equal to Him." Thus, to ascribe divinity to other than Allah, to claim that there is will other than Allah's, is to detract from the omnipotence of the Absolute Factor, to claim an autonomy and independence which denies this highest and noblest of truths. Even worse, it creates a division, a duality—because it implies separation. It promotes the myth that the Absolute Factor is distant and separate from the relative existence of all things.

We could say, if we really mean Totality, that either everything— including every man, including you and me—is divine or else nothing is, depending on our interpretation of the word "divine".

Either we are all "sons of God" or none of us are. It is simply that there are degrees of realizing it and a man who has fully realized it—a Moses, a Buddha, a Jesus or a Muhammad—has, through elimination of self-will, aligned and reunited with the Absolute Factor, or whatever we choose to call the Totality.

Of course, a part cannot be separate from the whole. It is impossible to "reunite with the Totality". This is the mystery, the enigma, the paradox. Believing ourselves to be separate from the Totality is an illusion.

*

43

We created man. We know the promptings of his soul, and are closer to him than the vein of his neck.

(*Qur'an, Surah 50*)

*

Muhammad recited his expression of Allah's Will throughout the twenty-two remaining years of his life.

Read literally, the Qur'an is a strange mixture. It could be said, by today's standards, to be dogmatic, enigmatic, over-dramatic, fantastical, repetitive, boring, out-dated, contradictory, intolerant, mundane, naive . . . Given the political and economic circumstances of the time and place of its origination, anyone could be justified in thinking that it is a first class piece of rhetorical propaganda, which, delivered by a suitably ambitious orator in a world where desert living was hard and precarious and where numerous factions competed for survival and supremacy, could have been skilfully used for personal power-seeking and security of leadership amongst a volatile and superstitious population. It has all the right emotional ingredients for firing and swaying an impressionable audience eagerly on the look-out for a cause and a leader who could wrest for it a better and richer living.

It paints an attractive future for the believer—a paradise of hedonistic luxury, especially for the men—and a fearful punishment of hell-fire and torment for the unbeliever on the inevitable Day of Judgement. It portrays a fierce and jealous God (almost spiteful on occasions) who wreaks terrible vengeance on all who do not believe and obey the law. And we find set down a good deal of the law to be followed by the faithful—laws pertaining to moral conduct, social administration and religious practice, including duty to parents, control of carnal desires, legislation for usury and division of inheritance, rules for wives, husbands, divorce, fasting, alms-giving, and so on.

In other words, for one who is prepared to become a Muslim, it provides him with an all-inclusive guidance and regulation necessary to live securely from cradle to grave (even though some of the instruction concerning the inferiority of women, how to be fair to

44

several wives, and permissible fornication with slave-girls is hardly relevant today).

On the other hand, for one who wishes to consider the Qur'an a little more deeply, certain difficulties arise.

*

Let us take one such problem, one with considerable implication, perhaps the fulcrum of the whole Muslim faith.

Every section or *surah* of the Qur'an is prefaced by the Statement: "In the name of Allah, the Compassionate, the Merciful . . ."

And yet, in section after section of the text, there are explicit assertions and examples of Allah's seemingly inexhaustible powers of wrath, vengeance, violence, punishment, torture, and so forth.

Hardly the behaviour, one would think, of one who is compassionate and merciful!

Ah, but of course, it must mean then that his compassion and mercy are reserved for the believers and all the terror is the penalty for failing to believe?

That might be logical. But what then are we to make of the following:

"The man whom Allah guides is rightly guided, but he who is led astray by Allah shall surely be lost . . ." (Surah 7);

"But Allah leaves in error whom He will and guides whom He pleases . . ." (Surah 14).

This would seem to suggest that Allah rewards the believer and punishes the unbeliever, even though it is His Will that the unbeliever does not believe!

How do we unravel that enigma?

It is just such a problem that gives the teachings of Muhammad its character.

We have now touched again on "the threshold of the unknown"— that aspect of deep religiousness which transcends all forms of religion, all human explanation, all justification by man's mundane standards, all intellectual logic—where experience and understanding are essential.

45

We are touching on the "heart" of Islam and the meaning of Faith; the prelude to Love.

As best we may, we have to consider "will".

By whose will does everything take place?

Islam will say, "By the Will of Allah alone."

So, we might well ask, do we not have will of our own?

It depends, as ever, on who or what *we think we are*.

If we think we are separate, autonomous beings then we may well, *by our standards*, think Allah unfair, illogical, or whatever.

But if, by surrendering our belief in a separate and independent self-will we inevitably surrender the belief in our ability to judge by our relative and conditioned standards, who then are we to say what is unfair or illogical?

*

If I think and believe I know who I am, then I will exert my will to maintain that status—and will suffer the "hell-fire" consequences of doing so.

But Allah is compassionate and merciful.

By His Will, self-will may be surrendered.

*

If all the trees in the earth were pens, and the sea, with seven more seas to replenish it, were ink, the writing of Allah's words could never be finished. Mighty is Allah and wise.

He created you as one soul, and as one soul He will bring you back to life. Allah hears all and observes all.

Do you not see how Allah causes the night to pass into the day and the day into the night? He has forced the sun and the moon into His service, each running for an appointed term. Allah is cognizant of all your actions, for you must know that He is the truth, while that which they invoke besides Him is false. Allah is the Most High, the Supreme One.

(Qur'an, Surah 31)

46

VII

Muhammad is called "The Prophet", which means that he was a man who "revealed God's Will".

We could take this in two ways: the first, the commonplace, that he related what God's Will was or is for man, for the world, or whatever; the second, the mystical, simply that he demonstrated what "God's Will" means. And by "God's Will" is not meant some separate, super-human force exerted by some extra-terrestrial agency somewhere "out there", not a will superior to that of any other creature, including man, but that *all* will *is* the Will of Allah, human or otherwise. All will, all natural law, is exercised by the incomprehensible Absolute Factor, the Most High, the Supreme One.

This is an extreme, difficult and uncompromising concept . . . because it requires the surrender in mind of any claim to independent self-will.

Any attempt to wrestle with it, compromise with it, justify and explain myself in relation to it, would itself be due to "self-will"!

It is not a case of Allah's Will *and* mine.

It is not even a case of me being willing to surrender my will . . . that again would be a self-willed action . . . willed by Allah.

It is a case of it being revealed to the mind that there never has been nor will be a separate and partial will. There is only One Will, and that is Allah's Will.

"My" separate will is an illusion . . . an illusion willed by Allah who "leaves in error whom He will and guides whom He pleases."

47

"But," my mind objects, "I decide things . . . I choose things . . . I determine to do this, that or the other . . ."

Do I?

Or is the decision or choice simply the "mind-computerized" result inevitably emerging from conditioned and memorized experience reacting to present circumstance? The "programming" of the mind is continually changing, of course, with the in-put of more experience, more learning, and with greater or lesser capacity for intelligence or wisdom, a factor often affected by the added ingredient of emotion or feeling—love, hate, anger, fear, terror, and so on. Occasionally I will excuse the choice or decision—"I was carried away", "It was taken out of my hands", "I really had no choice." Or someone else may see fit to excuse me—"Temporary aberration", "Balance of mind disturbed", "He didn't know what he was doing." And so on. But usually I claim the decision or choice as mine.

And because the ability to act and speak with so-called self-will is closely associated with my identity and assumed status, I am very loath to admit that really I did not will it at all. I am afraid to accept that I had no say in what happened. If I do admit it, where does that leave "me"?

If, in reality, I have no will of my own, what am I?

A machine? A process?

Yes, I may have to admit that.

So what difference is there between this human being and, say, a dog or a rabbit, a flower or a fly, a computer or a car?

I have a degree of consciousness which allows me to observe myself as a machine or process or whatever.

I have the ability to be aware of what is going on.

I can observe the Will of Allah . . . which embraces all will, mine included.

So who am I?

Paradox . . . Impasse . . . Perplexity . . .

And yet there is a way out of this labyrinth . . . by under-standing . . . if Allah wills it.

48

But the strange thing is . . . I am only aware of the way out when Allah has already willed it.

When I am aware of The Quest, I am already on it.

*

Let us see if we can very simply trace what has happened in our lives.

Long ago we were born. "Long ago" because we cannot experience or comprehend periods of time. "Long ago" is as long or as short as we care to tell. The number of years are meaningless in our experience *now*. It was, as it were, "once upon a time".

By whose will were we born?

Our bodies grew.

By whose will did our bodies grow?

At some later point in chronological time, we became conscious of ourselves—each one aware of himself or herself.

By whose will did we become conscious?

As babies, we automatically took action to attract pleasure and avoid discomfort and pain.

By whose will did we do that?

And as children, when we became aware of ourselves, we started to be able to work out with intelligence how to attract more pleasure and how better to avoid discomfort and pain.

But a momentous change took place at this point. Becoming conscious of ourselves and identifying ourselves as particular persons associated each with his own body, we began to think and say, "I *will* do this" or "I *will* do that."

As I conceived of myself, I claimed will as being mine.

Don't we all at this point assume will to be ours, and think and speak of it as such?

By whose will did we come to do that?

*

From that juncture onwards, will is assigned to a thousand thousand creatures, all apparently independently willing their own

49

actions. We think of anything taking action as having its own will.

And of course we exercised our wills as we explored the possibilities and the limitations of our talents and abilities—our physical and mental attributes.

At first we apply this will primarily in terms of physical pleasures and we direct our mental powers in the interests of attracting maximum pleasure in these terms. It is a time of trial and error, and our "memory-store" programmes our "mind-computers" accordingly. Success and failure, even with "the best will in the world", seem largely out of our control. Strength and beauty are attributes which open many doors; weakness and ugliness severely limit the available sphere of activity, our "territory". (And by whose will, we might ask, are we either strong or weak, beautiful or ugly?)

But as our mental powers mature and we learn our lessons from study and experience, so the power of will increases. Intelligence and other mental capacities and practical skills can begin to compensate for physical disadvantages. According to how intelligent and otherwise talented I am, so I can widen the territory in which to exercise my will. On the other hand, if these attributes are again flawed or weak, then my territory and the area in which to test my will are accordingly reduced.

By whose will are these strengths and territories determined?

I may begin to sense the power of being able to impose my will on those who are weaker. But, in my exchange with the world, in my effort to do what I want to do and avoid doing what I do not want to do, I will undoubtedly meet with opposition. My will is challenged and tested each time I experience a conflict of wills.

We can see that will—whatever it is—is crucial to success or failure in the world's terms. But where does it come from? How can I obtain more of it?

What wills me to breathe? Me?

What wills my heart to beat? Me?

What wills me to wake up and move through each day? Me?

What dictates the strength of my will to survive? Me?

What decides when I will sleep and when I will die? Me?
Even if I commit suicide, who wills that?

*

No matter how successfully or otherwise I manage to exert "my will" within the sphere of my activity, and no matter how large that sphere is, I am sure to have to acknowledge that it has finite limits.

I may well stubbornly or fearfully ignore the fact, but I have to admit that the assumption that I shall be able to continue my activity is precarious. A thousand forms of catastrophe could curtail it at any moment. Even if I am the most powerful man on earth and I exercise my will over others in a thousand different ways, I can never have the power to will it to continue even for one minute. If I do happen to think that I can, then that is the gravest and most foolish error.

How wisely or foolishly men exercise their so-called wills is not our concern here. What we need to focus on is not only the fact that our will is tightly circumscribed by hazardous factors outside our control but also, if we calmly and honestly contemplate the phenomenon, we cannot, in any real and secure sense, claim to have wills of our own—otherwise we would be able to *will* what *will* happen in the future . . . even one moment hence.

What actually happens is that in response to ideas in the present (which come from where and by whose will?) and in response to desires in the present (which generate themselves in our bodies and minds by whose will?) and in response to present events in the circumstances surrounding us (the majority of which are outside our control, no matter how much we may like to think we manipulate them), our intelligence decides on a course of action (or, possibly, no action). Having computed that response from all the factors, we then say, "I will do this" or "I will not do that." I claim it to be by my will that I behave as I do.

But what *really* dictated the course of action?

*

51

In itself, in the everyday traffic of life, it may be harmless enough to speak of "my will" and "your will", and in a thousand trivial matters our intents are fulfilled in fact.

But what will be crucial to my happiness, especially in more important and serious matters, is whether I really *believe* that it is my will which accomplishes.

If I do believe I actually possess an autonomous and independent will, then I will have to face the consequences. If I think myself responsible for my happiness, then I must accept that I am responsible for my suffering. If I claim that success is my achievement, then failure is my fault. I may even have enough confidence in my will to take on the happiness, suffering, success and failure of others also.

Fair enough. Maybe I think it right to take on that responsibility. But it will have to be within my limited sphere of operation. It will be a full-time occupation and a continual effort, stress and strain. And there are no guarantees. It will be an open-ended endeavour throughout the finite time of my life. And I will have to be prepared to accept that I will never be able to rest in the achievement of permanent happiness or success. Whilst I think it is up to me, I will always be vulnerable to the reverse that the next moment may bring.

And what in the end does it all lead to? An appreciative epitaph?

What am I doing it for? Who is keeping account of my efforts?

What is the purpose of it all? A death with no blame nor regret?

So is it really valid to maintain the belief that I have will of my own?

*

Even if I have confidence in my own will, I have to admit that it is limited and tenuous. It can be sapped by all manner of illness. If the body falters, the mind is threatened. Disease and accident can at any time disperse my will and unconsciousness or death will eliminate it all together.

What is more I will have to reconcile my will to better my

52

situation and the situation of others with the wills of others who wish to exercise theirs in ways at variance with mine. Above all, I will have to reconcile it with whatever it is that imposes on man the danger of war, plague, earthquake, fire, storm, senseless violence and collective madness—all manner of disaster that threatens to annihilate human will like a candle flame extinguished by a hurricane.

In other words, if I have autonomous will, then everyone else does as well. Result: discord and violence.

And if I have autonomous will, then there would seem to be an Almighty Will as well which can play havoc with my intentions, "good" or "bad". Result: anxiety and fear.

*

Here again, we are touching on the essence of Islam.

What is "will" and who has it?

Islam would say that Allah dictates the movement of every single atom of the universe. The power and the law by which everything moves is itself the Will of Allah and it is Allah's alone.

Having said that, it then depends on human intelligence to comprehend the statement, its meaning and implications.

A man may think he has autonomous will, independent of God. It is Allah's Will that he should think so.

A man may think he has no will of his own. It is Allah's Will that he should think so.

A man may think that there is an almighty god who alone has all will. It is Allah's Will that he should think so.

It is Allah's Will that every man desires, thinks, believes, speaks and acts as he does.

It is Allah's Will that a man should believe in God and it is His Will that another man should not.

It is Allah's Will that a Jew believes in Judaism, that a Christian believes in Christianity, that a Buddhist believes in Buddhism, that a Hindu believes in Hinduism . . .

There is no way out.

No compromise.

Except Islam . . . surrender.

There is no escape; no exception whatsoever. The Totality is an intelligent and utterly lawful system. And the mind of man can thrash about as much as it pleases—it will never find or prove a will of its own.

Ultimately, inevitably, when all the explanations have ceased, only Islam . . . submission.

Thus Islam transcends all forms of religious belief . . . since all belief (in the sense of giving credence to a self-projected concept or image) is derived from illusory self-will.

*

But Allah leaves in error whom He will and guides whom He pleases.

*

As we have suggested, it is all-important as to how the mind comprehends this matter of will. That is to say, it is crucial that the intelligence has the flexibility, perseverance, tolerance and "space" to go to the limits of the mind's understanding. If it once adopts conclusions and opinions, if it weakens and settles for apathetic acceptance, if it excludes, if it gives in to the narrow or small-minded, then there is trouble.

For at the primitive or ego level, the above surrender seems fatalistic in the extreme. It looks like an invitation to irresponsibility, to an orgy of self-indulgence, *carte blanche* to do just as you like. Or it looks like a recipe for stagnation, apathy, chaos and anarchy. No doubt it can easily and mistakenly be taken at this level, and has frequently been so, thus giving rise to what we may condemn as excesses of self-indulgence leading to inhuman violence, brutality, cruelty and indifference. This of course is a total perversion of truly religious "surrender". (And it is surely because of this potentially dangerous misunderstanding and abuse which could lead to social disintegration that the Qur'an goes to such lengths to lay down the rules of moral conduct and social behaviour?)

54

On the other hand, pursued intelligently and in a truly religious sense, the injunction to surrender self-will is an invitation to freedom. It calls for the highest and noblest sacrifice and responsibility —"response-ability", the ability to respond to Will, as opposed to bondage to supposed self-will. Once the honest aspirant has abandoned claim to autonomous will, there is true freedom . . . for the spirit is only bound by the belief in free-will. "Free-will" does not mean licence to do as one pleases; it means Freedom under Will.

This is yet another paradox in the enigma of existence!

To put it in other words:

Man is *bound* in suffering by the belief that he has *free*-will.

He is *freed* through the realization that he does *not* have *free*-will.

The Will of Allah first binds and then frees him.

*

It is here that we really come to grips with the question of religion.

Believing in self-will, we seem to separate ourselves from each other and appear wilfully to separate ourselves from the One Totality. In the dispersal of the illusion of separate will, we become "*bound* back" (Lat: *re-ligio*) to the Oneness . . . "God" by whatever name.

*

Perhaps again paradoxically, it requires greater strength to abandon self-will than to maintain belief in it. It is harder to "give up" than to "give in".

Why?

Because, as we suggested earlier, self-will is intimately bound up with self-identity. To give up self-will is to give up all concept and belief in "me". Surrendering separate will is to sacrifice myself— a kind of deliberate or conscious "suicide". (This has its ego-level echo in literal, physical suicide—which is self-willed, self-indulgent surrender in the form of self-destruction, when carried out in desperation, "without hope".)

*

Who creates "me"?
I do. Allah does.
Who sacrifices "me"?
I do. Allah does.
Who am I?
Who is Allah?
How are they related?
By "the flight of the unknown to the unknown . . ."
Allah is One, the Eternal God . . .

*

Muhammad, a man in history, used the word "Allah" to represent "the unrepresentable"—the Ultimate Principle, the Absolute Factor, the One Totality, call it what you will.

Thus we may see that he had no quarrel with true Jewish, Christian or other faith—nor any other true expression of religiousness. "Religiousness" is a state of mind that applies universally—to any man. Particular men express it in particular ways and thus are created particular forms of religion. But religiousness itself is "beyond form" and is essentially transcendent, not a matter of intellectual debate nor outward performance.

Today we hear much talk of the established forms of religion seeking to "achieve unity", which is to imply that unity can be created from separate parts. But where do the apparently separate parts come from in the first place? Unity is only "absent" for those who think and believe themselves separate, for those who ignore the fact that apparent separation takes place from and is subject to, already-existing unity. Unity is always there—as the prerequisite of illusory separation, which arises through self-claimed exclusivity and particular identity.

*

As expressed through Muhammad, the condemnation in the Qur'an is of the unbeliever, no matter what religion he happened to claim to belong to. The unbeliever in these terms is thus anyone

56

who believes that he has self-will. Thinking he has a separate and autonomous will, he thinks he can choose to believe in this or that form of religion, this or that concept of God.

If man thinks he can choose to believe in God or not, then he deludes himself. God is not dependent on either the wilfulness or the willingness of man!

Allah wills whether a man believes in God or not.

And then punishes him if he doesn't . . . so that he will understand the Will of Allah.

The paradox is that in reality man is never separate from the Totality, from God. There never was and never will be autonomous will . . . because it is inevitably derived from the Will of Allah.

Only in realizing so, can man understand and trust the compassion and mercy of Allah . . . and accept that inevitably Allah must "leave in error whom He will and guide whom He pleases."

*

God one day said to Moses in secret: "Go and get a word of advice from Satan." So Moses went to visit Iblis and when he came to him asked him for a word of advice. "Always remember," said Iblis, "this simple axiom: never say 'I', so that you never may become like me."

So long as there remains in you a little of self-love you will partake of infidelity. Indolence is a barrier to the spiritual way; but if you succeed in crossing this barrier a hundred "I's" will break their heads in a moment.

Everyone sees your vanity and self-pride, your resentment, envy, and anger, but you yourself do not see them. There is a corner of your being full of dragons, and by negligence you are delivered up to them; and you pet them and cherish them night and day. So, if you are aware of your inner state, why do you remain so listless!

(A story from The Conference of the Birds)

VIII

Words and their interpreted meanings are at one and the same time both liberating and binding, both clarifying and confusing.

And we are limited by the laws by which we structure them into phrases and sentences at the same time as these conventions allow us to communicate and understand each other.

And we are limited by our conditioned powers of conception, imagination and belief at the same time as they allow us to explore and cope with the mystery of our existence.

Allah leads into error whom He will and guides whom He pleases . . .

Our being led into error is in order that we may understand what it is to be guided.

*

As we have already intimated, in so many words, what seems to bedevil our yearning for understanding, our longing to comprehend and relate to the Absolute Factor so that our lives may have order and purpose is that we are led into the temptation to conceptualize—to conceive of "God", as something "other" than ourselves.

By tracing back through the process (which is the principal value of memory, as opposed to the idle use of it—nostalgia, dwelling on past mistakes, cancerous resentment, regret, apparently missed opportunities and so on), we may recall and observe what has happened.

The body is born into the world and is given a name by which to identify it.

It grows up and at some moment in time self-knowledge or consciousness emerges—"I become aware that I am me."

What does that signify?

"I"—spirit, consciousness, the Self—"enters" or "arises out of" the body, and mind becomes aware of the presence of this named person here, "me".

"I am William Corlett" or "I am John Moore"—by whatever name, "I" become "me", this physical entity.

And here is the crux of the matter. "I" becomes identified with, synonymous with, involved with the body which "I" have come to inhabit. This "I"—the essential principal, the spirit, the consciousness, the central core or reference point of this being, the absolute and original factor of this person here—becomes identified with a particular, physical entity in finite existence. "I" believe the Self to be "me". The subject becomes the object.

Fair enough. We all do it. And it would seem to be right and proper that we should, otherwise we cannot function properly in the world.

And maybe that is enough. Maybe we could leave it at that and simply live out the appointed finite span believing ourselves to be particular physical entities. We can enjoy the pleasure that comes our way and suffer our allocation of pain and discomfort and hope for the best when death approaches. But many are not content with that. They may not use these particular terms, nor necessarily be aware of what they are doing, but in different ways and to some degree the majority in modern "civilized" societies attempt to disengage the "I" from the "me". All forms of escapism in all manner of guises represent this process. It may simply be indulgence in glamour fantasies, the dreams of fortune, the vicarious emotions of entertainment, all kinds of investment in exaggerated pursuit of worldly possession, travel for the sake of it—in a thousand ways it is possible to find relief from "being me". Or, in a more desperate degree, it may be recourse to alcohol or drugs—whatever "artificial" and accessible means are available to facilitate "forgetting me". And then, in even more extreme cases, those which end up in the care of mental institutions, there is a partial, temporary or total "abandonment of me". In its various forms, "schizophrenia" represents a forced schism between the "I"—the essential core of spirit of the person—and the physically existing entity called "me". The ultimate in wilful severance is suicide. (All these forms of wilfully contriving unconsciousness are of course distinct from nature's provision of relief—for example, periodic sleep, the ecstasy of Love and Beauty, natural death, and so on.)

In these varying degrees of wilful relief from, forgetting and abandoning "me", a disintegration takes place, both in the individual and, according to the number of individuals involved, then also of society itself. We could say that to the degree we fail to take responsibility for ourselves, so, individually and collectively, disintegration takes place.

So why, by the Will of Allah, are we led into this error (assuming we suspect that something has gone wrong!) and what is the error?

*

Perhaps because, through being confused (having "fused together the 'I' and the 'me' "), we have elided the subject with the object. We have believed that we have will. The responsibility has been ignorantly transferred to "me"—that which cannot possibly cope with it.

The effect is that the mind then thinks "it is up to me" to sort it all out.

"*Always remember*," *said Iblis* (*Satan*), "*this simple axiom: never say 'I', so that you never may become like me.*"

. . . "I" may never become like "me" . . .

*

The trouble is that, if the illusion of self-will becomes widespread, men collectively take it upon themselves to believe that they can sort out the world's problems in the world's terms. Of course, we must endeavour to resolve problems—but only in the Name of, and in surrender to the Will of, Allah. Once people believe they themselves have autonomous will, so arises, for example, the materialistic, communist state. Eventually and inevitably, such a state *must* self-destruct.

*

The confusion and perplexity, and at times desperate suffering, arises because "I" (the subject) believe that "me" (the object) can find the way out. Thus I invest myself with self-will, which is an illusion.

"Me", this particular person here, cannot, and never *will*, find the resolution—except through inevitable disintegration and death.

Thus the error lies in expecting "me" to find the answers. And because "me" cannot do it there results the attempt at irresponsible relief, forgetting and abandonment.

The key is not "out there". I will not find the resolution for myself in the phenomenal world. The key lies in remembering the subject, the original and real "I".

Who remembers?

Who am I?

The experience of desperation is not really the "me" (who is a fiction) trying to find relief or escape but the "I" wishing to withdraw from belief in "me" in order to realize or know itself.

Once the "I" has entered the body and has enabled it to mature and take its place in the world, the "I" then begins to try to withdraw; "I long to find the way back whence I came."

In the process, "God becomes evident to Himself."

*

Then the Answer is: I mean that thou, in thy stages of drawing nigh and of being far off, wast not a thing beside God (whose name be exalted) but thou hadst not the "knowledge of the soul", and didst not understand that thou art He without thou. Then when thou art united to God (whose name be exalted)—that is, when thou knowest thyself—thou understandest that thou art He. And thou wast not aware before that thou wast He, or He other than He. Then, when the knowledge

61

comes upon thee, thou understandest that thou knowest God by God, not by thyself.

(*Ibn 'Arabi*)

*

Allah guides whom He pleases . . .

Perhaps then we may see that this does not necessarily mean that some capricious deity is playing a life-and-death game with us but that he who is pleased—by the meaning, comprehension or experience "Allah"—is inevitably guided.

The word "please" is derived from a Latin root meaning soothe, calm, appease or reconcile.

Thus Allah "leaves in error whom He will", which is to say that the wilful mind is inevitably left in error in its belief in "me" and "my will" but that if the mind acknowledges there to be no self-will, no "me", it is then eased and reconciled.

He who is in error is not aware of Allah and is left so.

He who questions his situation is already "turning towards Allah".

Or, in our earlier terms:

If I am unconscious of there being a Quest, then there is no Quest.

If I am conscious enough to be questioning, then I am already on The Quest.

*

He who is questioning is already "turning towards Allah", experiencing the "I" which is the spirit or consciousness in himself seeking resolution or reconciliation . . . "The flight of the unknown to the unknown."

Oddly enough, "resolution" is both a determining to do something (will required) and the dissolving or ending of something (no further will required).

*

It is thus the acknowledgement that self-will must be abandoned that "turns" the mind toward "Allah" . . . towards "God" . . . towards religion.

The question is then how this surrender is to be accomplished. In terms we used earlier, how is the mind to comprehend and relate to the Absolute Factor?

And we may suggest that this is the subtlest and most disciplined of undertakings.

The difficulty is that once the "I" has, as it were, elided with "me" (the physically existing object) then "me" becomes the subject in relation to the apparently separate world "out there". Hence it will become customary to use the term "I" when referring to the body-identified person here. Perhaps unfortunately, because in English we write as we do, we always use the capital "I" when ideally, in order to indicate this particular person here, we might better use the small "i". (For example, "i am here" just as "you are there".) The principal "I", which is the enlivening spirit or consciousness of Self-hood in every man, is the one and only "I"; but when using it in relation to this person here, it is as it were only a small and particular manifestation of it, an "i".

Nevertheless, ultimately, and in contradiction to the above, when it is revealed that all will is the One Will of Allah, then it is seen that the apparently separate "i"s are an illusory fragmentation. It is perhaps indicative of the intelligence of the formulators of the English language that the small "i" was never introduced as the first person singular pronoun but always the capital "I", even though in ignorance the full significance of its singularity is commonly taken in vain and error. Ultimately, the "I" must be One and Alone.

Hence, in the story quoted at the end of the previous section, the best advice is "never say 'I'," meaning that, if it is not yet known "who I am", it is foolish and deceptive to pretend that it is known.

*

The point is that because it is assumed *by me* that "I" am this separate, body-identified and particular person here, and have become used to thinking of everything else as being separate from "me", then "I" am always taken to be the subject in relation to all else as object.

Hence, when introduced to the god-idea, what happens?

The mind takes in the idea and tries to conceptualize it in relation to myself.

Immediately, the conceptualized "god" is thought of as an "object".

Because I am a self-contained entity here, then "god" must be elsewhere.

How is this "god" to be imagined?

Well, of all the images available and experienced in my life, this "super-intelligence" cannot be less than man himself (i.e. we are not likely to think an animal image, for example, as being appropriate). So, since we are not able to imagine an image we have never seen, the best we can do is think of this almighty deity as some kind of super-human, with man-like attributes and characteristics (and preferably only exhibiting the benign side of human behaviour—kind, loving, merciful, forgiving, rather like an ideal parent).

We cannot here consider all the varieties of image that have been used throughout history and they are, in any case, not relevant to the theme. It is simply that attempts have been made and are made (and we were probably not discouraged from doing the same) because of the habit of objectifying in relation to ourselves and in our own terms. Hence the temptation to give an anthropomorphic image to this mind-projected almighty being.

This may have been appropriate and inevitable for the primitive (either for ourselves as children or in less developed societies) for it helps to have something imaginable to worship but it is not an occupation that appeals to the awakening intelligence. It is too obviously crude and self-deceptive.

So, without recourse to an acceptable form or image, how is the mind to fulfil its desire to conceptualize the "god"?

64

Well . . . perhaps vaguely as an invisible, intangible, formless power or being . . . or something along those lines.

But is this really satisfactory either?

It is again somewhat nebulous and it is asking rather a lot to expect me to worship "it" and pray to "it" and so forth when I am not allowed to think of "it" as an "it", an object with form.

If there is, within, the desire to serve other than myself, to give up self-will in deference to a higher will, to believe in other than myself and to worship other than myself, then the confused mind naturally thinks that this "other" must be "something" or "somebody".

And how are we to speak of this "god"?

Since we are considering such a super-intelligence, it would hardly be appropriate to use the term "it". Therefore, since it is man's preoccupation and we have only two further third person singular pronouns available, then it will have to be "he" or "she", and the former traditionally has the priority so . . . the "god" is commonly referred to as "he".

The above may seem glib and simplistic (and possibly blasphemous to the already committed believer) but it is the kind of commentary and explanation we have to resort to once we have assumed autonomy as separate physical beings and have assumed the habit of objectifying everything, including "god". And this is where "religion" is in difficulty.

How to teach about "god" and avoid the error of saying or implying that "he" is an "object" in relation to all human beings as "subjects"? How to "turn this upside down" to convey that "he" is the One and Only Subject in relation to which we are all "objects"?

(It was presumably in recognition of the fact that Allah cannot be "taught" that Muhammad forbade "priest-interpreters". In Islam, in surrender, each man is in direct relationship with Allah; no other man can possibly "stand between" as intermediary. And this again demonstrates why Muhammad is regarded as a "messenger" and not one who taught this or that about "god".)

How can "god" be conceived of without projecting or inventing "him" and dreaming up all kinds of attributes and characteristics about "him"?

Not only is it impossible but it is what Muhammad might have called the temptation to fall into "idolatry". Idolatry, in this comprehensive sense, means worshipping any mental concept as well as physical image (which is why he forbade the use of any representational divine image in human form).

*

Of course it is "better" that men should worship a "god"—that is to say, some transcendental concept "outside" themselves. It is better that they should do that rather than worship themselves or any "thing" else. Through god-idea indoctrination, the religion in society can help disperse potentially explosive and anarchic self-indulgent behaviour through propagating and maintaining rules of moral and social conduct appropriate to the character of the "god". Although the religion may be on the wane and declining in influence, the legacy of these rules is well-embedded and serve to stabilize the society long after the original inspiration has faded.

But what remains is only the visible tip of the iceberg, as it were. It is the outer manifestation or the external application appropriate to the "religion". Correct speech and behaviour is not so much a matter of learning and conditioning—although it may have to be in the initial and preparatory stages—as the natural conduct of one who is truly religious, one who has truly surrendered to the Will of Allah. You can tell someone that he should love his neighbour and he may well think he cannot do so. Nevertheless he may well obey to the best of his ability and at least on the face of it behave towards him as if he genuinely does. That helps. But for him actually and naturally to be able to do it requires a "religious conversion within". And that is not a matter of his willing himself to do it; it can only be done by the surrender of self-will, the acknowledgement of the Will of Allah.

*

For, as we have suggested, surrender to the Will of Allah is not a case of forcing or suppressing self-will, nor even of diverting it into more laudable pursuits. It is a matter of conversion, where belief in self-will is totally abandoned.

As we have also suggested, this surrender of will is not by default an invitation to irresponsible fatalism or self-indulgence. This surrender means *no* self-will—the elimination of that which interferes with the ability to respond selflessly to the needs of man and the world. And, again, this does not necessarily mean going around "doing good" all the time. It is always a matter of responding appropriately to the immediate needs of the immediate circumstances as they *reveal themselves* and are understood by the individual at the time—not in accordance with how I and others think and have been led to believe things ought and ought not to be. All too often this can be a diversion of self-will, a bolstering of the ego.

*

What then if there is cessation of objectifying "god"?

Immediately there can be no divisive concept of "man here" *and* "god there".

It cannot be "me" *and* the "god" whom I worship, pray to, believe in, and so on.

With clear abrogation of self-will, "me" is eliminated, as also is the projected "god-idea".

Only the One Totality remains.

In that surrender, only God is.

God . . . by whatever Name . . . is the All.

Who then am "I"?

"I"—the spirit or consciousness in myself—is not known as an "object". "I" is the subject, the witness.

The mind acknowledges that "I" cannot be known by it, as an object.

The mind acknowledges that "God" cannot be known by it, as an object.

It simply acknowledges the presence . . . of both?

But are there two?

If neither can be known as "objects", how could the mind distinguish between "I" and "God"?

Is not "God" what the mind comprehends as the spirit, the consciousness and the substance of All? And is not "I" what the mind comprehends as the spirit, the consciousness and the substance of this person?

Are they therefore not the same, inasmuch as they are not distinguishable?

Where do I come from at birth? Where do I go to at death?

I . . . God . . . "the flight of the unknown to the unknown."

*

. . . But you must know God by Himself and not by you; it is He who opens the way that leads to Him, not human wisdom. The knowledge of Him is not at the door of rhetoricians. Knowledge and ignorance are here the same, for they cannot explain nor can they describe. The opinions of men on this arise only in their imagination; and it is absurd to try to deduce anything from what they say: whether ill or well, they have said it from themselves. God is above knowledge and beyond evidence, and nothing can give an idea of His Holy Majesty.

*

In this understanding, the emphasis changes in religious practice.

Worship is then not *of* something, but the mind's disposition to surrender self-will. ("Worship" derives from "worth-ship"; hence the making of the mind to be worthy of obeying the Will of Allah.)

Prayer is then not petitioning *for* something *from* someone but, again, the disposing of the mind to abandon self-will. (In this sense it is essentially an invocation, the invoking or "calling in" of Will.) For example, it is not that some "god" can be entreated to send peace by the pleading of human beings; simply that through surrender of self-will on a large enough scale peace is inevitable.

Belief then is not that there is "a god out there somewhere" but a being free "*in* God", a trusting by mind within the Totality.

And faith, again, is not put *in* some "thing" but *is* what remains when trust is *not* put in any "thing", which includes ideas, theories, concepts, beliefs, assumptions and opinions.

This abandonment of belief in the validity of self-will is a long process requiring constant vigilance and perseverance because, needless to say, self-will takes many subtle forms and guises, and the mind is continually led astray and into compromise.

And, perhaps the most difficult aspect of it, there is no reward for "me". That is extremely hard for me to accept, accustomed as I am to expecting pleasure and consolation as the result of my efforts.

*

What is more, my mind is so used to being able to formulate through will and imagination its goals in the world that it is reluctant to accept that it cannot expect anything of this undertaking. (Which is why perhaps, the world is apt to call such aspirants "fools", "idiots of God" and the like.) There is no future in it for me. Over and over again, each time the mind falls into temptation to gain for itself, a thousand times a day, it is, relentlessly . . . surrender now . . . surrender now . . . surrender now . . . until surrender for ever.

The result (if we can even call it that!) is beyond the mind's comprehension. There is only a "knowing" that in the surrender there is the under-standing of the Will of Allah. In this act of pure self-sacrifice, requiring faith and the unconditional "love of the lover for the beloved", there arises comprehension of relationship to the Absolute Factor.

*

What does all this imply?
That "Man" is "God's Mind".

*

Through our learning we become so used to conceiving of and dealing with "things" that we are apt to be discomforted by "nothing". As it is said, the mind abhors a vacuum.

Although we frequently use the word "nothing" we rarely consider its full significance.

Somewhere, sometime, back in human history, someone comprehended the abstract; the absence of all things; the possible origin or substance or resolution of any manifest thing; that which contains or is beyond the totality of every thing—no thing, nothing.

When we really contemplate the phenomenon, it is an awesome and extraordinary leap of intelligence for the mind to be able to consider NOTHING.

Why should man in particular be able to comprehend the possibility of an absence of everything?

It is an extremely rich and revolutionary idea. It is so powerful, magical and mysterious in its implications that there could be books written about NOTHING.

Could it not be essentially and inextricably linked with the ultimate in human achievement—man's understanding of himself?

Is it not from the perspective of the unknown, the nothing, that he is able to consider the totality of the finite everything?

What is it that enables him to postulate the possibility of the infinite—not infinitely "small" nor infinitely "large" nor infinitely "long" nor infinitely "short", because no matter how extreme there would still be finite measurable dimension—but infinity itself, space without limit?

Might not the comprehension of NOTHING indicate an expansion or release of consciousness, one peculiar to man as far as all creatures on this planet are concerned?

Might it not be crucially connected with religiousness?

*

Whoever first did it, how astounding that someone expressed this comprehension by the drawing of a circle.

If you were to sit down and were to try to think of a way to represent your comprehension of NOTHING—with its properties of totality, all-containment, infinity, and so on—could you find a better one than a circle?

We call this symbol of a line without beginning or end "a circle" and we use it to denote a vowel, a letter, a number and "an exclamation expressive of sudden feeling".

It is the Arabs who are credited with first having used it as a "number" representing absence of anything, nothing or zero. At first, this may seem an odd thing to have done since numbers are, on the face of it, just a device for counting, and you cannot count nothing. But maybe (in fact, surely) they must have realized that in understanding the existence of all countable things, nothing has to be taken into account as the perspective from which all things are accounted.

Otherwise, who counts the first "one" . . . ?

*

We can begin with the finite, the totality of all things, the One. But where does that One come from?

Must it not have to be preceded by the unknown infinite out of which it originated—what we may call NOTHING?

The causative factor, the Absolute Factor, which is the prerequisite of all finite, temporal things, cannot itself be a "thing"—otherwise it would be formed and created. Therefore we need the formless, unperceivable Factor, the NOTHING, as the before-the-beginning, the beyond-of-the-continuing and as the after-the-ending.

. . . He begot none, nor was He begotten. None is equal to Him . . .

So how does He communicate?

Through His Messenger.

*

71

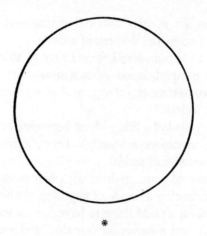

*

O . . .

O my heart . . .

O my heart, if you wish to arrive at the beginning of understanding . . .

IX

Space.

What experience does the word "space" call to mind?

What is space?

". . . continuous extension, viewed with or without reference to the existence of objects within it . . ."

Infinite NOTHING?

". . . interval between points or objects viewed as having one, two or three dimensions . . ."

The fourth dimension itself—an infinite space-time continuum?

These are attempts at formulating in words the ultimate "circumference" of the mind's experience.

But, of course, that limit cannot be described or defined.

Extending out from the vague and unlocated "centre" of our being, attention flies to the furthest definable edge of the known in a kind of mental space exploration and the "inner eye" of imagination looks out beyond, to the unimaginable unknown.

". . . the flight of the unknown to the unknown . . ."

*

For practical purposes, when we have become body-identified here on earth, we tend to make use exclusively of the secondary definition of space given above—the interval between objects. It is the relative meaning of the word, synonymous with the measuring of distance between known objects. It represents the degree of separation of one relatively dense object from another. But it is secondary because the separation is illusory; in reality the two objects are together and inseparable in the same space-time continuum.

Because there is no apparent practical use or purpose in the primary meaning—the continuous extension, viewed with or without reference to the existence of objects within it—it has been largely ignored and has played little part in the majority of human lives throughout history (although it has always been essential, in other terms, to true "religiousness"). However that situation is now changing—and maybe we can catch a glimpse of the imperative importance of true "religiousness" now, regardless of the terms we each may care to use in our experience of understanding it.

The psychological evolution of man—the evolution of his consciousness if you like—has now reached the point where the primary meaning is becoming more and more insistent and significant, beckoning him to either wisdom or madness on a scale hitherto "unknown"—a universal scale.

The crucial point is how he is responding to it, *with* or *without* reference to "the existence of objects within it".

Increasingly, man is behaving collectively. With the development of mass communication, the tendency to larger groupings increases also. Politically, socially and economically, the small group and the individual find it more and more difficult to remain independent and self-sufficient.

This process of centralization or universalization may be either positive or negative; it depends on whether it takes place *with* or *without* the reference to the particular "objects" within it.

Negatively—"without reference"—we may see the process of agglomeration as inimicable to the individual when the larger and larger groupings, taking on a "mad" collective will of their own (Allah's vengeance), frequently aided and abetted by scientific and technological "advances" mindlessly undertaken "for the sake of scientific advance itself" begin to reduce the human being to the role of manipulated object. The symbol *par excellence* of the negative aspect (of Allah's vengeance) is the emergence of the weapon of mass-destruction.

Positively—"with reference"—we may see all collective attempts to achieve equality, fairness, widespread education, co-operation, aid and welfare as altruistically motivated mass developments, hope-fully in the interest of the individual's well being. But are they? At a practical, material level they may occasionally be so; but how well does collective will cater for real individual need?

Why then, in this process of "continuous extension with or without reference to the existence of (individual) objects within it" is there a commensurate and growing instinctive fear and despera-tion in the private individual?

Because the negative aspect is becoming a tangible and real threat whilst the countering positive aspect is continually faltering, falling short, going astray?

Why the latter?

Because no matter how positively motivated in relation to his fellow men, if the purpose, however vague, is to sort out the world's problems for *Man's* benefit, comfort and survival, then it can never succeed.

Because, as we have said, in reaching for the primary definition of space ("reaching for the stars") *there is no practical purpose.*

If the negative aspect prevails, there will be mass destruction—plenty of relative space remaining.

If the positive aspect could prevail, there would be unlimited, mass procreation—with a commensurate decreasing of relative space.

The former would be sudden annihilation, the latter gradual "suffocation".

The trouble is that the weapon of mass destruction is an im-mediate and real menace, whilst the Utopia is an elusive dream. No wonder that there is mass anxiety and widespread dissatisfaction. "The devil and the deep blue sea."

*

Is there a third possibility?

Is there a way out of this dilemma?

Yes.

It is through a transcendent understanding of space—for which there is no definition in the dictionary—the "Islamic" space.

75

There could not in fact be a definition of it, although we might define it "negatively" as that which is evident when all definable concepts of space are abandoned—the NOTHING.

This third possibility is the truly "religious" . . . the transcendent . . . apparent through surrender of self-will . . . acknowledgement of the Will of Allah . . . the revelation of the Allah purpose (of no practical use to physically existing and surviving man) . . . but, at the same time, the fulfilment of man's purpose . . . "out of this world" . . . the realization of the Truth of Man's estate, with no earthly application for man the creature.

Curiously—but, of course, inevitably once law, the Will of Allah, is seen revealing itself at all levels of consciousness down through all levels of matter—the current symbol of this third possibility, the "escape" alternative, is represented by man's new-found ability to "fly into space". We may certainly question what practical purpose for earthly application can result from this activity. If it is simply to further "continuous extension", to extend his own survival-space, then ultimately none at all. (But what it may represent as an analogy or symbol of his "higher aspirations" we shall touch upon further in the second part of this book.)

What more appropriate representation could there be of "the flight of the unknown to the unknown"?

*

Arising out of the duality and tension of one unknown and a second unknown is the knowledge of space or unlimited volume, called by the ancients "the ether", "the shining or burning substance of reality". In other terminologies it has been called by manifold names—the Infinite, the Absolute, Nirvana, City of God, Kingdom of Heaven, Promised Land and so on.

But who goes there?

Here the intellect falters in explanation.

How can there possibly be *two* unknowns.

By definition, no matter how far the known is extended, the unknown remains singular, aloof and unaffected.

And, yet again, the intellect confounds itself and words fail.

For what divides the known from the unknown?

By extending the known, do we imagine that the infinite and unquantifiable unknown is reduced? Can there ever be a sum total of the known and no unknown remaining?

The known may appear to extend or expand, but does that make the slightest difference to the unknown?

Known and unknown, finite and infinite, time and eternity—these are not extensions or dualities at the same level. They are not opposites. They belong to different dimensions. The known, the finite and the temporal are mental concepts; the unknown, the infinite and the eternal are inconceivable.

Allah is One, the Eternal God. He begot none, nor was He begotten. None is equal to Him.

*

What is going on?!

I wake up to being here on this earth and am led to believe that this person here is me—an autonomous, self-contained creature. I could just accept that fate and settle for my natural life-span before disappearing as mysteriously as I arrived.

But then I start experiencing these extraordinary questions asking me who I am and what I am here for and so on.

What are they doing?

Provoking me to try to understand something?

Are they messages of some sort?

Who is the messenger?

By whom are they sent?

Where do they come from?

They suddenly manifest in the mind—some in response to what is going on around me but some, the metaphysical ones concerning the mystery of my existence, seem to come from "out of the blue" . . . from "inner" or "outer" space . . . from nowhere.

Really—if I honestly stop for a moment to consider—where *do* these questions come from?

Usually I am just aware of questions after they have occurred and I simply get on with trying to answer them, sometimes to my satisfaction, sometimes not.

But what an extraordinary question it is in itself: "What *is* a question?"

*

If we do contemplate the question of questions, we may realize something else, also extraordinary.

It would seem that my whole potential for development is dependent on questions.

And if I am not to remain merely an automatic response-mechanism then especially important are the questions I ask myself about myself.

Who am I?

Why am I here?

What is the purpose of my life?

What happens when I die?

If I make no attempt to answer these questions, what possibility is there other than to accept my fate as a physical organism, no matter how successful or otherwise my performance during my life-span in the world's terms?

Or, to put the proposition above the other way round, what would happen if there were no questions?

*

All the way from the most trivial to the most profound, questions enable us to bring intelligence to bear on the desires and fears arising within us. "How can I best fulfil this desire for pleasure?" "How can I best avoid that threat of suffering?"

I depend on asking myself questions in a thousand different ways if there is to be any improvement on sheer passive acceptance of what happens to me. If I do not question, I am simply at the mercy of each passing desire and threat and never have the opportunity to do other than respond mechanically and predictably to each arbitrary stimulus.

This statement in itself prompts questions of a different calibre.

Am I simply a vehicle for experiencing and responding to desire and threat and is my sole function then the relieving (or re-living) of those desires and threats?

Is that all I am?

Or is there more to it than that?

The fact that we can respond to such questions is the product of a consciousness peculiar to the human creature on this planet. So far as we can tell, other creatures do not ask themselves questions.

But where do the questions come from?

Is the ability of man to conceive and formulate questions due to his being conscious of and receptive to a dimension denied to other creatures?

Further, could that consciousness be the further dimension itself . . . a dimension that the mind, dealing in the terms of the three-dimensional phenomenal world can only call the "unknown"?

Must not a question come from the "unknown"?

How could questions arise from the "known"?

In becoming conscious of himself existing as a three-dimensional creature, Man looks at it himself, as it were, from a dimension beyond, the unknown dimension.

In asking himself the questions, Man *reminds* himself.

The mind does not know who is asking but the questions provoke the mind to remember. In this process the mind is being asked to release itself from commitment to the limitation of three dimensions only. In comprehending the unknown dimension, the mind remembers and realizes the full measure of Man . . . remembers God, Allah, or the Unknown by whatever Name.

And this takes place in the transcendent "space", the ether, beyond measurable distance and chronological time.

Hence mind experiences questions instantaneously. Consciousness of a question is immediate. It may take the mind time to formulate it in order to speak it but it is "heard" by the mind or "known" by the mind in a kind of timeless moment of conception. The passive "womb" of the mind is impregnated by an active

79

introduction from a dimension outside itself, an "unknown father". The mind may then succeed in allowing the question to develop and formulate; but if the mind is not mature enough, the question will abort. If the question is properly formulated, then it may be made manifest or be "born", by being thought or spoken.

If the question is formed and manifests without flaw, then it contains within it its own immediate answer. The "truth is born" and is comprehended by mind in "no time at all". Thus it is that revelation or realization is instantaneous, a "divine intervention", a "message from the gods".

*

What "space" is there between the known and the unknown, between Man and God?

What "time" is there between the known and the unknown, between Man and God?

No distance.

No time.

Here and Now.

*

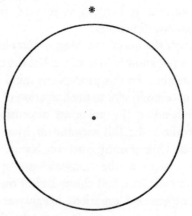

It is the experience of this mind that "I" am somehow, somewhere, the centre of this being here, and that radiating out from it is "my" world, the sphere of experience of this being.

That sphere has no known limit—for can I know the measurable perimeter of my mind?

But does the centre uphold the circumference or does the circumference dictate the centre?

Put in rather crude and simplistic terms, is my sense of being the centre due to the world being around me or does the world appear to be around me because I am here at the centre?

*

What *is* the centre of my being?

Is it something—a locatable thing?

Where is it?

Where is the centre of the universe?

Where is "my" centre in relation to the centre of the universe?

Could it be that my centre *is* the centre of the universe?

Why not?

Where else could the centre be . . . in the experience of this person?

But then, you might well object, you are therefore also the centre. And there cannot be two centres of the universe.

Fair enough.

But, again, how do we conceive of the centre?

Is it actually possible in the terms of three dimensions to locate that point which is the centre of my experience of the universe or the point which is the centre of yours?

A centre is a point which by definition has no dimension.

If it has no dimension, how could it possibly be located?

Only by reference to a known circumference.

And can we define the circumference of our experience of the universe?

Since our experience of the universe has no defined limit and we cannot therefore locate the perimeter, the centre, which has no known dimension or location, can be anywhere and everywhere *at the same time*.

Both you and me are the centre of the universe simultaneously . . . as is everyone else.

And if the centre is anywhere and everywhere, what "space" can there be between the centre of you and the centre of me?

And what "space" can there be between the unlocated centre and the unlocated circumference?

Now we are touching on the mystery.

There is no reality in the belief that space separates objects. There is no reality in the belief (based on the belief in being the body-identified object) that you and me are separate. The centre of your being and the centre of my being are the same unlocated point which is at one with the universe. The centre, being everywhere, is not separate from the circumference.

This means that there is no space in existence.

Space does not *exist*. How could it? If space existed it would be measurable.

Or, we could say, space is "beyond" existence . . . in another dimension.

But here words fail us because "beyond" immediately implies distance . . . an imagined projection from this vaguely body-identified centre.

The best we can say is that space is the non-existing in which there is existing . . . and yet they are not separate.

Space is the NOTHING which subtends everything . . . where the centre and the circumference are the same.

Are we now closer to God?

Have we ever been separate from God?

Who is there beside God?

Is this how the mind comes to believe *in* God?

It cannot be any other way.

Believing in no separate thing . . . believing in NOTHING . . . is inevitably believing, to be living, *in* God.

*

Allah is One, the eternal God. He begot none nor was He begotten. None is equal to Him.

*

Does this give us a glimpse of mystical understanding?
God does not exist.
"He" does not *exist* in this world as a "fact" . . . in the way that you and I think we exist as phenomena, along with the mountains, the trees, the seas and the stars.

"He" is THE NON-EXISTING the One and Only SPACE . . . the ubiquitous, unlocated centre that is everywhere and nowhere, containing the Totality of All.

Could this be right?
Could we surrender to this Islamic Space?
We would have to give up all we have assumed and relied on in order to make this awesome leap out of the familiar . . . a "space-flight", with no known destination, to the outer reaches of Mind.

Would we have the courage to abandon the finite, three-dimensional facts of our world to reach for the unknown which is unknowable?

These are questions that only I can answer when mind has been prepared to admit them.

This is where we close with the profound meaning of faith.

*

If the faith is there, what does it require that I should do?
Sacrifice.
Once the mind is convinced that our relative and temporary existence will not satisfy our deepest questions, then we have no option but to sacrifice our illusory purposes and concerns and follow where the questions alone will lead us.

To the degree that we are prepared to abandon the false will we have the faith to surrender to the Truth.

The poignancy abides in the realization that we cannot have it

83

both ways. We cannot retain the "known" *and* aspire to the "unknown".

How could *we* cross the non-existent "space" between them?

How could *we* know how to discover the unknowable?

No matter how much is known we would be no nearer to the unknown.

*

What is faith?

That which remains when all belief and self-will are surrendered.

How can we have it?

We cannot have it. It is there when we have ceased to look for it or to claim it.

Where does it come from?

It does not come from anywhere. It is there always, revealed through self-sacrifice.

Man is drawn to God by His Will . . . not ours.

The Love of God is beyond understanding.

If we will understand—stand under Will—the Love is apparent of Itself.

*

What is Love?

No separation.

No space between.

*

Physically—once I have become body-identified as this person here—I might say that my skin defines the limits of my portion of space. And likewise, you could say the same about "your space".

Due to learning to assume that I am my body and you are your body, we come to believe we are separate, with "space" between us.

That is why, when we are *in* love, we wish to touch—to dissolve the apparent separation.

*

84

And mentally?

I might say that my eyes and ears reach to the limits of "my world" at any given moment. And you could say the same about "your world".

Although we might say that my body is mine alone and yours is yours alone, it seems that "my world" overlaps "your world" when we are together. Because it appears that we share the world, I assume that the world is not mine and thus that it is separate from me. Likewise, the same applies to you.

But, when we are together sharing the world, in what measurable and locatable terms are our minds separate?

We may think we are "of two minds" but where really is the perimeter of my mind and the perimeter of yours?

Do our minds occupy separate or common space?

When we are *in* love, are we not "of the same mind"?

*

Most of the time, we accept, believe and act as though we are separate from each other and from the world.

It is this fundamental belief which is at the root of all our aloneness and incompleteness.

What we experience as being in love are those moments when the veil of apparent separation is withdrawn.

Love and separation are the two sides of the same coin.

I can only experience love because I have believed myself alone and separate. And I can only experience aloneness and separation because I have experienced love.

*

What is the ultimate separation . . . of which the earthly experience of being in love is but an echo?

What is heavenly or ethereal love ("ethereal" being of the ether)?

Could it be the removal of the veil of separation which apparently divides the known from the unknown, the existing from the non-existing, Man from God?

How could such a separation be resolved finally by anything less than death?

Would that mean that death is the final consummation of love?

*

Is not death only feared because it appears to be the final confirmation of separation—the annihilation of "me"?

But supposing, during life, there is the surrender of self-will, the conscious sacrifice of all claim to my independence and automony—is not that also "the death of me"?

What is the difference between the two?

*

Those unprepared for death regard it negatively—with fear or resignation or as welcome relief from suffering. Those truly prepared are said to regard death positively—as a final consummation of love, the realization of the Union of the Lover with the Beloved, the "I" with "God".

*

As we come to the end of the first part of this book, we could say that we have driven intellect hard. We have pursued logic to the point where it defeats itself.

Perhaps we could say that intellect proves to itself that it cannot prove anything. In so doing it has served its purpose and can only surrender its will to explain and justify.

Has it any further use?

Yes—as guide to the "heart".

For once love is released, the "heart" can be foolish. It can fall into idolatry.

In its wilfulness, the intellect interferes with and blocks emotion and feeling, causing all manner of anxiety and stress.

Under Will, intellect reminds the heart of the Source and Goal of Love. Otherwise the heart falls over and over again into error of worship.

The true longing is for God alone.

But Allah leaves in error whom He will and guides whom He pleases.

*

How else is Mind to comprehend the Love of God if it is not as God Loving Himself through Man, His Messenger?

*

Muhammad's message, the Qur'an, reveals the Will of Allah.

The intellect can find no compromise with it on my behalf; Islam, surrender, is the only course.

Perhaps we can justifiably conclude that, if it is the message of "The Last Prophet", there is now no space for argument left.

There is now only "the flight of the unknown to the unknown" . . . perhaps "on the wings of love".

(Which is perhaps why, after the time of Muhammad, there was heard increasingly the ascetic, mystic message of Sufism and there emerged the wealth of Islamic poetry, music and song concerning love.)

*

Do we experience longing in the heart?

Do our hearts cry out for the consummation of love which will disperse our aloneness, incompleteness and ignorance forever?

How will the journey be?

*

O . . .

O my heart . . .

O my heart, if you wish to arrive at the beginning of understanding . . .

Part Two

I

We, whoever we are, came at birth from the unknown. And after we had arrived we grew accustomed to the world and made it familiar. And having made it familiar, we became busy in it, thinking we knew who we were, thinking we were separate from each other, striving and surviving, trying to love each other.

We found that life in the world was not easy. We were looking for happiness, understanding and security—but though we had fleeting moments of success, they did not last. If we had been able to find permanent fulfilment of those desires, the world would have been a different place. But . . . that is not how it was. For all our attempts, we never managed to allay the haunting fear of aloneness, incompleteness and death. Even when we invented "God" as a way out of our difficulties, it did not suffice. "He" was only a cipher endowed with powers and attributes through our imagination. Even though we tried hard to believe His Presence and obey His Will, we were still fearful, earth-bound mortals.

So was that to be the end of it?

A hopeless and helpless journey through life filled with meaningless activity?

It might have been so if we had not heard the question—that mysterious message that sounded with increasing insistency.

Who am I?

I did not know where the question came from nor who asked it. But I was being spoken to, and I heard.

And I began to search for the answer.

And that answering was the first step on the journey . . . the beginning of the return to the unknown whence I came.

*

Even a journey of a thousand miles begins with a single step.

*

And so we take the first step and the journey begins. It is always beginning . . . every moment, every day, every life.

We may not know what it is that we are looking for; we may not know where the journey will lead us, nor even be sure about where it is that we are setting out from. We only know that we have taken the first step in search of the miraculous.

*

Why am I searching?

Perhaps it would be as difficult to answer this question as it would be for a salmon to know why it will use up every last ounce of its energy, pitting its strength against a mighty waterfall, intent as it is on the spawning pools high in the mountains; or for a bird to know what prompts it to embark upon the hazardous voyage of its migration, flying thousands of miles—drawn towards its "unknown" destination in the warm lands.

If I am honest with myself it is something like that.

I have started on the journey because, for me, the journey is there to be taken.

*

If I cannot say what it is that I am looking for—then the *finding* becomes of secondary importance to the *looking*; and this, perhaps, is the key to the enigma.

I now understand that whatever I find on my journey into the unknown then that will not be "it". Why? Because any "thing" that I find and claim, I will immediately make *mine*. Man, having gone to the moon, having stood on the moon, having returned with "moon rocks", has turned the moon into a satellite of the earth.

The moon has lost its mystery and turns out to be a dry "earth" of dust and rock—in man's estimation. Wherever man goes, wherever I go, I will make what I find into some "thing" in my estimation.

What I am looking for is that which is beyond my estimation.

*

What is the spur to my undertaking the journey . . . the real poignancy of my aloneness, incompleteness and insecurity?

Fear of death?

Do I know—*really know*—that one day I will die? All the evidence points to the fact that this is so. But do I really know it? Is there fear of death in me?

Is there *fear* in me?

Do I take the next step because of fear? Fear of not moving; fear of not reaching my destination; fear of not fulfilling my potential?

If I do not know how or when my death will come—how can I make any provision to avoid it?

So it is with The Quest.

I may study books, enter a religious order, assume disciplines and practise constant prayer and meditation—and in doing so, I may tell myself that I am making the right effort to attain my perfect goal. In this way I will believe that I am the master of my destiny and that it is through my effort that I will one day realize the sublime Truth and the eternal Love.

But how can I take aim at the unknown, the unseen?

It is like shooting an arrow in the air. If there is no target—then, wherever the arrow lands, that is the bull's eye.

If I am not aiming the arrow—and yet the arrow hits the bull's-eye . . . do I shoot the arrow—or is it drawn to the goal of itself?

So it seems with The Quest.

All that is necessary is that the arrow is in the air;

All that is necessary is that the journey is being taken;

All that is necessary is that The Quest exists.

*

Watch yourself walking . . . not in a mirror, but with "the mind's eye".

Walk very slowly.

What moves the foot?

What is "walking"?

Why is there walking?

Who is walking?

Who is watching the walking?

The watching with "the mind's eye" and listening with "the mind's ear" is the first step into the unknown . . . the Islamic Space.

Don't let us ask now why we take the step. Nor even how we take it.

Let us rather have faith to take that first step—knowing not where to go, but observing simply that we are going . . .

So journeys begin.

So The Quest is observed—by the end of the journey, if there is to be an "end", much may have been revealed.

In the past the search has sometimes been called the "search for the miraculous".

The first miracle, when it is really seen, is that first step.

*

The truth has come, and falsehood has vanished away: surely falsehood is ever certain to vanish.

(*Qur'an, Surah 17*)

*

Mantiq Ut-tair, "The Conference of the Birds", was composed in the twelfth century by the Sufi poet Farid ud-Din Attar. It is an allegorical, or symbolic, poem which tells the story of the journey of the birds, as they set out on the pilgrimage to the court of the *Simurgh*, the Great Bird.

The final purpose of the birds on their journey is union with God.

It is a delightful work of literature which has been translated into many tongues. It can be read as a story, rich in anecdote, both amusing and serious; or as a philosophical work, outlining the precepts and teachings of the Sufi tradition—that mystical expression in Islamic terms of truly religious surrender of self-will.

In other words, *Mantiq Ut-tair* is either a book that you pick up, perhaps read, digest and enjoy and, when it is finished, put back on the shelf; or it is a book that, as you read it, may change your perception of life, revolutionize your beliefs and alter the whole direction of your existence.

Has any book such power?

Only if the knowledge is within it and it is revealed through "the mind's ear".

Only if the knowledge is in the reader, so that he recognizes the message.

*

We have seven valleys to cross and only after we have crossed them shall we discover the Simurgh. No one has ever come back into the world who has made this journey, and it is impossible to say how many parasangs there are in front of us. Be patient, O fearful one, since all those who went by this road were in your state.

The first valley is the Valley of the Quest, the second the Valley of Love, the third is the Valley of Understanding, the fourth is the Valley of Independence and Detachment, the fifth of Pure Unity, the sixth is the Valley of Astonishment, and the seventh is the Valley of Poverty and Nothingness beyond which one can go no farther . . .

(*The Conference of the Birds*)

II

The mystical journey . . . "the flight of the unknown to the unknown" . . . the flight out into the "timeless" and "spaceless" fourth dimension . . . a journey on which "I" set out in any moment, now, abandoning "me", the earth-bound creature . . . a journey from which, one day, "I" will never return.

For "the time being"—whilst there is still "time"—the body remains on earth and "I" occupy it and take responsibility for its maintenance and activity. During those periods, there is historical time and three dimensional space and "I am" here, existing.

When the journey is undertaken, now (when "I" am not here) "I" am in realms of eternity, infinity, Islamic Space. This absolute does not co-exist with the relative, the particular, the separate; when "I" am "of it", all these illusions do not exist.

*

A challenging . . . baffling . . . inspiring . . . frightening . . . crazy idea?

Maybe . . . but can I ignore it?

I could not be concerned with the "unknown" all the time, any more than I am constantly concerned about what lies beyond the earth's atmosphere, what the stars are or what lies beyond the farthest reaches of deep space. Such considerations come and go as fleetingly and as spasmodically as the weather changes and the clouds cross the sun.

Most of the time I am busy "getting on with life". But as the years pass by and I grow in experience of my earth, so a dullness overcasts my life. I behave and react in an increasingly habitual and

94

set pattern. I buy and sell, get and spend, rise and fall, witness hopes fulfilled and hopes disappointed. Always there is a new horizon for me to strive towards, always there is a new desire for me to work towards. I form relationships and see them lose their vividness and become part of my habitual existence: I seek new stimuli and having found them I make them part of me . . .

As within, so without: as below, so above.

The world has now been explored, there is nowhere left to discover. This does not mean that men have been everywhere—nor does it suggest that I would not be stimulated or entertained by going to some of the places that I have not seen before. But the pioneer spirit on earth is now denied to man. There is nowhere left to discover: not on earth, on my earth.

The only mystery left is further and further "within"—as for the scientist who probes the "inner" worlds of space with his microscope. Or further and further "without"—as the astro-physicist explores the mysterious realms of outer space.

Man needs the mysteries more than he realizes. And it is surely no mere coincidence that as "universalization" takes place on the planet earth and man takes his first step out towards the stars so, on a scale perhaps unprecedented, human psychological evolution reaches for the fourth dimension—for the eternal and the immortal, the "outer space" of his mind.

*

Modern space technology developed a threefold vehicle.

The first, a massive "physical" rocket, is required to provide the propulsion to overcome the gravitational pull of earth and to "escape" beyond its atmosphere. When its work is done, it is discarded.

The second part of the vehicle is then used to carry and guide the mission on course in order to arrive in an orbit of the final destination. At the same time it carries a communication system to keep in touch with earth. This part of the vehicle too could be discarded if there were to be no return journey.

And the third part, the landing vehicle, is the most refined—equipped with sensitive instruments to investigate and interpret the new world.

Finally we should not omit to consider the purpose of the threefold vehicle—to carry man himself out into space.

*

But what, it is worth enquiring, is Man hoping to find out in the vastness of space? What is he looking for?

Is he looking for something? Or is the main purpose to go and find whatever there is to be found for its own sake?

A flight into the unknown.

So far the information that is being brought back is rather mundane.

The moon has been found to be a dead rock; not surprising, that is what it was always expected to be. But the planet Mars—where once it was believed there could be a species of life similar to our own—has now been examined, photographed and probed by satellite and Mars turns out to be . . . dust and rock, ancient and "dead".

The possibility would seem that wherever we look we will find the same "deadness" and the haunting probability of Man being entirely alone and isolated in the universe grows more acute and more poignant.

Only wise men and fools make journeys into the unknown.

Man's ventures into "space" would seem so far to have been the brave attempts to provide himself with reassurance of his own wisdom. Of course there is a natural curiosity; of course the achievements have been remarkable; of course travelling into space has been an awe-inspiring, technological miracle. But the limitation of the whole performance stares out at us; ultimately, and in what real terms can it be said to have been "successful"? Is it foolish or wise?

We have built our three stage vehicle and it has worked. If and when we can afford it, we will now be able to go on building bigger and better vehicles for exploring space as "the interval between points or objects". But why? Simply for the sake of exploration? To extend man's territory? Or in order that man may "escape" the earth and its laws into different realms of space as "continuous extension" and time "as eternity" where he may become physically immortal? What is the point of this endeavour if we do not consider "the fourth stage"—Man himself? Who and what is he?

The space vehicle is a useless toy unless the creator of it understands his motives. Our vehicle may eventually be able to take Man to Mars; and then perhaps beyond to the further planets and then . . . perhaps to another galaxy and the infinite silences of nowhere.

But—and this is the real challenge, and perhaps the point where our analogy is stretched as far as we can take it—this will require a certain "sacrifice". For he will eventually come to a juncture where a space-travel journey will be proposed where it is known that the travellers will not be able to return to earth.

Imagine that. Would you be willing to undertake a journey knowing you will never come back?

*

It is Man's infinite possibility that he may know himself.
Know thyself.
But the requirement for doing so is that he sacrifices or discards all that he has falsely believed himself to be.

Like the space traveller, if he wishes to cling to his earth-bound status as a creature and continue as an earth creature out in space, his journey remains forever confined to the Valley of the Quest.

The first part of this book might be said to lead us to the limits of the earth's laws and atmosphere. At that juncture, intellectual explanation, as the boosting power, has to be discarded as a vehicle capable of explaining the journey in logical and "earthbound" terms.

The second stage vehicle takes over. It is a new beginning in the Valley of Love . . . on the 'inner space' journey to the *Simurgh*.

*

I was on that day when the Names were not,
Nor any sign of existence endowed with name,
By me Names and Named were brought to view
On the day when there was not "I" and "We,"
For a sign, the tip of the Beloved's curl became a centre of revelation;
As yet the tip of that curl was not.
Cross and Christians, from end to end,
I surveyed; He was not on the Cross.
I went to the idol-temple, to the ancient pagoda;
No trace was visible there.
I went to the mountains of Herat and Candahar;
I looked; He was not in that hill-and-dale.

     .   .   .   .   .

I gazed into my own heart;
There I saw Him; He was nowhere else.

                        (*Divani Shamsi Tabriz*, Jalalu'd-Din Rumi)

III

Another bird said to the Hoopoe: "Tell us, O you who wish to lead us to the unknown Majesty, what is most appreciated at that court? It is necessary when going to kings to bear precious gifts; only vile men approach them with empty hands."

The Hoopoe replied: "If you follow my advice you will take to the country of the Simurgh what is not found there. Is it fitting that you should take what is already there? True knowledge is found there, secrets are found there, obedience to higher beings is found there. Take then the ardour of love and the longing of the spirit; no one can offer other than this. If a single sigh of love goes to that place it will carry the perfume of the heart. That place is consecrated to the essence of the soul. If a man should heave one sigh of true contrition he will forthwith be in possession of salvation. . . "

(The Conference of the Birds)

*

So . . .

Let us begin . . . not from *the* beginning as a starting point in time, but from where we find ourselves *now* . . . in the ever-continuing beginning.

Is there ever *a* "beginning"?

Every thing is a direct result of some thing that came before it.

Thus today is dictated by what happened yesterday; our perception of any event is dependent upon some previous preparation; our birth is the consequence of our parents' lives and births . . .

This book is the outcome of a series of complex actions and interactions, spanning back through historic time. We, the authors,

D*

had to know each other well before we could collaborate, before we could be "of the same mind"; to know each other we had first to meet; to meet we had to be in the same place at the same time; to be in the same place at the same time was in itself the outcome of previous events . . . back and back . . . to the "beginning" . . . where?

How far back is this beginning?

If you take a pencil and a sheet of paper and you draw a circle . . .

As you are drawing there is a point where the circle "began"— the point at which the pencil first touched the paper . . .

But when the circle has been completed . . . and the "end" and the "beginning" are one . . .

Where is the beginning?

*

For me to exist at all as precisely the being that I am now—with this precise physical body, this precise age and so on, the fertilization of the egg within my mother's womb by the seed from my father took place at a precise instant. Moments earlier or later and perhaps—just perhaps—a wholly different being might have been created; or no being at all . . .

In other words my existence here in the world, which I take so very much for granted, is in reality the result of an incredibly fine coincidence—a moment, a timeless "now", in a ceaseless chain of action and reaction, of cause and effect.

Or, to put it in another context:

If the authors had begun writing this book a month earlier, or a week or even a day, an hour, a moment . . . would the book have been written in precisely the way it is being written? Would the same words have been used? Would the same ideas have been expressed in the same sequence?

What we may take as being the considered expression of a life-time's study may in reality depend upon a momentary random event . . .

There is a story about the poet Samuel Taylor Coleridge, hard at work in his study writing *Kubla Khan*—perhaps his most famous poem. There is a knock at the door and, history has it, a "person from Porlock" came to pay him a call. When the person leaves, the poet returns to his study . . . and the whole course of the poem is completely changed . . . for ever.

On such haphazard events does creation apparently depend!

What we may take to be the considered expression of a lifetime's work . . .

That which may have seemed crucially important a moment ago may be completely forgotten now; that which seems crucially important now may appear to have arrived in our consciousness as if from nowhere.

The writer may believe that he is developing a theme and that he "knows where he is going" but in all honesty he has no idea what words he will employ from beyond the present limit of his mind's vision . . . what will pass his "eye of imagination" from moment to moment.

"Mind's vision", "eye of imagination": I did not know that I was going to use those expressions, nor did they exist for me a moment before I "thought them" and wrote them down.

Where did they come from?

Where did they "begin"?

Were they waiting in some other realm, ready to drop into consciousness?

Are they fact or fiction?

In what respect do they exist?

Do they ever not exist?

It is only when my mind becomes conscious of them that they "fall into place", enter time and space. The fact for me is that *now* they are.

What we call a beginning is our sudden consciousness of the continuing.

*

And we can each experience this for ourselves in the act of speaking.

The next time you are having a conversation with someone, observe yourself talking; listen to the words that are being uttered through your mouth; try and catch the actual process . . . the arrival and selection of the words . . . as it occurs.

Do we consciously work out the words and then speak?

Or do the words literally "pour out of us"?

As we observe, it is as if we step outside ourselves into "outer space" and watch the words being spoken . . . as if the mind is itself "reciting" through the medium of the body's vocal mechanism.

Once one begins to home in on an exercise like this the observation can be unnerving.

For it appears that not only do we express ourselves in an amazingly haphazard and arbitrary way but also that that which is being expressed has its own capricious, immediate, unprepared quality . . . no matter how much we may like to think we are saying what we mean.

Other than in everyday, practical terms, how often do we actually know and say exactly what we mean?

And how often do we mean what we say?

And how precisely does another know what we mean?

We mean what we are—from moment to moment.

Whose ideas are we thinking and expressing?

Like a seed blown upon the wind, that which we are expressing is continually subject to the background variations of our emotional state which can change from moment to moment.

And when do we try the hardest to express what we mean and mean what we say?

When we wish to express the truth of our love?

When we wish to express the Love of Truth?

*

Muhammad heard a voice saying "recite".

The words that it is claimed he "recited" were later written down and became the sacred script of the Qur'an.

But let us remember that Muhammad himself did not write the words down.

He simply uttered—as you or I utter—the words seemingly coming from nowhere, forming and flowing, sounding and fading . . .

It appears that Muhammad was "talking to himself" but that those who listened to him decided that what he was saying was worth understanding.

What was it that he was saying? Did he know what he meant?

What were the first words that he uttered that are deemed "significant" to the Muslims? Did they know what he meant?

As has already been stated, neither of us, the two authors, are Arabs nor do we read or speak Arabic.

Presumably Muhammad did not speak English. So, if we had been present when he was "reciting", we would have found it difficult—impossible—to understand the meaning of his words. And if, further, we had no knowledge of the fact that there were other languages besides our own we might have been persuaded to believe that the sounds issuing from his mouth were gibberish.

This is the intellectual approach to the unknown. If we rely upon previous information for our understanding of a present event— what happens when we meet the "unknown" (that which does not connect with any previous experience)? We either dismiss it, and carry on as if it has not occurred, or we attempt to liken it to some other event in our experience and understanding—and either prove or disprove it. We try to make it mean something familiar to us.

Thus we by-pass what it really means *in itself*.

*

For if we return to the example of Muhammad speaking gibberish—because we don't understand the words—something else may come to light.

He is not only speaking words—he is making *sounds*.

103

The *sound* of the words may convey something very important.

Consider any conversation; is the overall effect that of a series of words following each other? Or is it not also a continuously flowing *sound*, formed and modulated by the silence or *space* between the words, by the variation of volume in the voice—by its light and shade, its timbre?

A conversation—or a speech—is a *musical* expression.

The music of the voice—or the harmony (or disharmony) between the voices—may tell the listener a great deal about a conversation, even if he cannot actually distinguish or give intellectual meaning to the words being spoken.

An angry conversation and a loving conversation have quite a different quality of sound; it is possible that the *sound* is far more evocative and informative to the listener than the words being used.

*

After you have had a conversation with someone, what happens? What remains or lingers?

You perhaps remember for some time later what was said, but what *really* mattered?

The emotional content and legacy of the exchange?

Looking back at the meeting, you may have a positive or negative feeling about it. Was it uplifting and happy? Or was it sad and depleting? Was it harmonious, constructive, useful to the further-ance of mutual understanding? (No matter how remote, still connected with the truth of love or the Love of Truth.) Or was it frustrating, bland, tense, discordant, angry? (No matter how remote, still a failure to express the truth of love or the Love of Truth.)

All the "things" of our meeting and conversation will be resolved, forgotten and fade away and are, in relation to our life and death, of no significance.

But the accomplishment or failure of harmony, little by little, furthers or retards the fulfilment of our lives.

*

Word-forms are to the "head" what sound is to the "heart".

Words are the language of the intellect, sound is the language of the emotions.

A sigh expresses a deep feeling for which no word can be an adequate substitute.

The cry of pain is not a word, but a sound.

And, of course, the words will probably come a moment later, if there is a listener.

The cry of pain informs the listener that there is anguish; but it does not tell the nature of the anguish; it cannot inform or instruct. It cannot guide the doctor to the root of the pain, nor the lover to the heart of the matter.

And as for a conversation, it would not be possible to have one without the head and the heart both being employed in the expressing.

*

The important thing is that they are *both* employed even though, as one may say, "my heart isn't in it".

But you can read a book without the heart being influenced at all.

A book may be nothing more to you than an intellectual exercise. It may not "touch" you. If it is such it is so for one reason; it lacks the *sound* to touch your heart. You can read the words and therefore interpret the intellectual message that the writer is attempting to express; but you cannot hear the voice through the writer's words.

Surely for this reason the art of writing poetry evolved?

Poetry communicates to the reader not only by using words but also through the special rhythm and meter of the juxtapositioning of those words along a line. In this way a *sound pattern* is established which is closely akin to music. The reader hears a "silent music" of the heart in his mind at the same time as he is intellectually understanding the words. The head and the heart are both occupied.

At its best poetry can link the reader to the emotional state of the writer at the time of the writing.

It is significant that the Qur'an is written in a poetic prose form.

(Did Muhammad "recite" in this poetic form? Perhaps we will never know.)

Here is a transfer of *Surah 1* from the Arabic into the corresponding English hieroglyphs:

Bismillahi 'rahhmani 'rrahheem.
El-hamdoo lillahi rabi 'lalameen.
Arrahhmani raheem.
Maliki yowmi-d-deen.
Eyaka naboodoo, waéyaka nestáeen.
Ihdina 'ssirat almostakeem.
Sirat alezeena anhamta aleihim, gheiri-'l mughdoobi aleihim, wala dsaleen.   *Ameen.*

And here is a translation of the Arabic "sound" into English "sound":

Praise be to God, Lord of the worlds!
The compassionate, the merciful!
King on the day of reckoning!
Thee only do we worship, and to Thee do we cry for help.
Guide Thou us on the straight path,
The path of those to whom Thou hast been gracious;—with whom thou art not angry, and who go not astray.   *Amen.*

*

This Surah, which is variously termed "the Opening of the Book", "the Completion", "the Sufficing Surah", "the Surah of Praise, Thanks and Prayer", "the Healer", etc., is repeated several times in each of the five daily sessions that the devout Muslim practises. Although most of us will be unable to sound Arabic fluently we may perhaps get a sense of the humming, chant-like quality of the original. Such sounds, repeated often within a short space of time, day after day, year after year, would clearly influence the mind—just as music can influence—or "pass through or over"—

the mind. Even at the least subtle level, the audible sound vibrations will have a physiological effect, ideally easing cerebral tensions.

Once the mind is "passed through", eased and stilled, the connection is re-established with the *heart*. In other words, the over-dominant intellectual process—that of trying to "work things out" is stilled, and the emotional reception, that of "feeling", is released.

This device of "chanting" is one used by many religious groups and we will return to it in more detail when we come to consider the phenomenon of prayer; all that need be said about it at the moment is that it is similar to singing and synonymous with music.

The word *music* is defined in an English dictionary as being "the art of combining sounds with a view to beauty of form and expression of emotion." The word *emotion* is defined as "a moving of the feelings: . . . feeling, distinguished from cognition and will".

*

. . . If a single sigh of love goes to that place it will carry the perfume of the heart.

*

"The Conference of the Birds" is just such a mystical *poem*.

It speaks of "the flight of the unknown to the unknown"; of the soul's longing for salvation; of the supreme desire of the individual to be united with God.

This book—in common with all the books in this series—is an individual expression on the part of its two authors; of their experience of this longing.

The first part of the book, like the first stage of space flight, is an attempt intellectually to lift us from the earth, from the limits of the familiar, from the restriction of belief and assumption.

Now we are travelling in a different context, a different "time" and "space", where the laws are different and logical structures will not suffice.

We are now having to use intellect "passively" or "negatively", to keep the flight—now powered by feeling and emotion—on course (not that we know the destination, simply that we know through discrimination when we are moving off course).

Here we will find great difficulty expressing in words what we may want to convey. There are no words that adequately describe the experience of emotions and feelings; the nearest we can ever get is through the art of simile and the likening of one state to another. Whilst we all share the earth-world, once out of its atmosphere there is no common ground. Here we become individual in a true sense, and alone in that no one else can experience for another. We have "companions" on the journey but we will not arrive by self-willed collaboration. Each has to find faith and trust that the unknown destination will pull or draw us through its own will or attraction. In this phase, things will "feel" right or wrong—even when they cannot necessarily be proved to be so.

But, some people may ask, why make such difficulties for ourselves?

If there are no words which will adequately convey the emotions, why try to?

Why not leave well alone?

Because we are on a journey and our goal is in the universality beyond the farthest reaches of particular mind. And by trying to express the experience we encourage, and are encouraged by, our "companions".

We are going beyond the "known"; there cannot be words for that which is beyond conception or before experience . . . the unknown.

Words, and the intellect, lift us to just this very point, the threshold of the unknown. Active intellect is the booster rocket that lifts us from the earth and sends us flying headlong towards a point of no return. The mind cannot know itself . . . but it experiences the longing for the truth of love and is motivated by the Love of Truth.

*

In this part of the book, we are using as our map, "The Conference of the Birds".

On their journey to the *Simurgh*, the birds, the companions, had seven valleys to cross.

These valleys represent the seven points of difficulty that anyone may experience who is genuinely set on the quest into the unknown.

Such is the nature of the "dimensionless space" into which we are entering that, mysteriously, much of the ground that we will cover will seem strangely familiar; the same and not the same; for, remember, we are travelling in a void where historical or sequential time is not a linear continuity and where space is not the measurable distance between three-dimensional objects.

Each of the valleys will have aspects that will be recognizable to us.

Recognizable—and yet seen or heard as if for the first time.

As though all our lives we had been seeing the world as a reflection in a still pool—and we are seeing it directly for the first time; or as though all our lives we had been listening only to the echo of the sound—and now we are hearing it directly for the first time.

This is how it works.

How do we know?

Partly from our own experience; each of us will find that we recognize certain aspects for ourselves; partly from writings such as "The Conference of the Birds". Such writings speak to the heart, and the heart, it would seem, *knows*.

There is nothing "new" in space; all that is new is *our viewing of it*.

Remember, each of us is the final, most delicate and most essential purpose of the space vehicle. We are that which observes. Given the right preparation it is as though we meet experiences that we have had many times before, but now we recognize (re-know) them; now we *see* them for the first time with our full potential; it is not the world that has changed—but *us*; for we now look back at the world, as if from outer space.

*

It is indeed "the flight of the unknown to the unknown".

But as we cross the seven valleys we will realize much *about* ourselves; and we shall see much that we have falsely believed *about* ourselves. It will not be an easy journey for we will see that all that false belief must be discarded. But, as the darkness of illusion falls away behind, so faith will strengthen and no matter how arduous, painful and baffling the journey, we will feel increasingly the pull of the destination (our destiny) as it draws us through the mists of uncertainty that shroud the mountains of difficulty.

This isn't a pastime or a hobby, this quest that we are on.

It is an all-consuming way of life.

As Muhammad began to recite he feared that he was going mad.

Let us take heed of the warning. Once we pass outside the earth's atmosphere and leave the familiar—who can say what is sane and what is insane?

What is "normal" in the void?

Normality is a constant reference to the past, how things *were* when we made them familiar.

In space there is no past, no time . . . the journey is *now*.

*

The Creator of the World spoke to David from behind the veil of mystery. "All that exists, whether good or bad, visible or invisible, moving or unmoving, is only a substitute if it is not myself, for whom you will find neither replacement nor equal. Since nothing can take the place of me, do not separate yourself from me. I am necessary to you, you are dependent on me. Therefore do not desire that which offers itself if it be not I."

(*The Conference of the Birds*)

IV

"When you enter the first valley, the Valley of The Quest, a hundred difficulties will assail you; you will undergo a hundred trials. There, the parrot of heaven is no more than a fly. You will have to spend several years there, you will have to make great efforts, and to change your state. You will have to give up all that has seemed precious to you and regard as nothing all that you possess. When you are sure that you possess nothing, you will still have to detach yourself from all that exists. Your heart will then be saved from perdition and you will see the pure light of Divine Majesty and your real wishes will be multiplied to infinity. One who enters here will be filled with such longing that he will give himself up completely to the quest symbolized by this valley. He will ask of his cup-bearer a draught of wine, and when he has drunk it nothing else will matter except the pursuit of his true aim. Then he will no longer fear the dragons, the guardians of the door, which seek to devour him. When the door is opened and he enters, then dogma, belief and unbelief—all cease to exist."

(*The Conference of the Birds*)

*

A pretty uncompromising "beginning" to the journey!
But let us consider.
If we pause for a moment, we may look back on our experience. If by accident of birth and family, we have or have not been given beauty, wealth, privilege or any other "advantage" in worldly terms, we come to assume our share as our standard. We take it for granted and come to base our attitudes on it. Once we have believed

our share is ours by right, the "pitch" of our sense of values is established.

Whatever one person's pitch or position is in relation to another or in relation to the average of his or her particular society and the world at large, it is never stable and invulnerable. The two possibilities in a world of ever-changing form and inter-change of energy, are an improvement or a deterioration of that position. To bring about the former and avoid the latter demands work and attention. Why work and attention? Because any living organism is a system of energy conversion. Inertia (as distinct from periodic rest and recuperation) means failure to convert energy into work and any organism experiencing increasing entropy will inevitably suffer atrophy. To put it in other terms, Allah destroys the useless. (After all, why should any system maintain that which fails to serve it?) Thus, given a certain status or position, it can be taken for granted in the sense that it has been given free of charge as a grant; but it cannot be taken for granted in the sense that there is no responsibility attached to it. It requires work to maintain and improve it; otherwise it will inexorably degenerate because it has, as it were its own in-built self-destructing mechanism. If we observe ourselves, our society and the world at large we will see the self-destructing mechanism in operation at all levels and in all manner of context where organisms fail to take responsibility for themselves or have passed their usefulness.

Of course, it has always been so and always will be so.

Allah leads into error whom He will and guides whom He pleases . . .

But as we have already suggested, it is now apparently happening on a scale hitherto unrecorded in Man's history. And as a symbol *par excellence* the weapon of mass destruction is a symbol representing the ultimate in self-destructing mechanisms as far as human life on this planet is concerned. It confronts us as an unprecedented challenge. Does it mean that Man is becoming useless?

We have assumed our status and privilege as creatures on this earth. Unless we wish to be destroyed as being no longer of use we had better cease taking our situation for granted. It cannot be a case of the world providing more and more of what we want; that can only lead to exhaustion and inertia. It is a case of work and attention to responsibility.

The question is: To what or whom is our responsibility?

*

From our given position we are influenced by an emotion with dual aspect. The *desire* for improvement or gain is inextricably interwoven with the *fear* of deterioration or loss.

Desire–fear. It depends on which of two views are taken of the same proposition. Both may be the spur or motive to work and accomplishment; both may be the seed of self-destruction.

Of what emotion are they the dual aspect or reflection?

Love?

Not love as romantic notion or sentimental attraction or idolization, which is but a small, flickering reflection of the flame, but the all-consuming fire which ultimately resolves creation itself—through destruction or dissolution, burning up both desire and fear.

Ultimately we will be destroyed by Love.

Either, through the wilfulness of self-love, our desires and fears will destroy us.

Or, alternatively, our desires and fears will be destroyed through purifying fire, and we will consciously and willingly self-destroy through surrender or submission to Love itself . . . Allah . . . God . . . whatever Name we prefer.

*

No wonder the beginning of the journey is uncompromising!

In the above context what else would we expect but doubt, difficulty, resistance, obstacle . . . "a hundred trials" . . . to work through in order to transcend our desires and fears.

*

But, again, let us consider.

Anything that we really want—we must want and work for to the

113

exclusion of all the other things that will prevent us gaining that one thing. It is always the way. We only really value that which we have earned.

At the most profound and subtle level most of us desire to go on living (if only through fear of dying). We therefore temper all our pursuits with this basic desire. In other words we will go to certain lengths to attain something but we will not put our continued life in jeopardy. However there are times when we become consumed by our desire or fear and our minds become confused. At such times it seems that we would "rather die" than not gain what we want or have to face the worst of our fears. In so saying, we acknowledge the desire to self-destruct.

The above refers of course to selfish desires and fears born of self-love. We have complementary altruistic desires and fears born of our sympathy and compassion for our fellow creatures. This is a step in the opposite direction—self-surrender through love. Taken to the extreme, we may be asked "to give our life" for a fellow human being, our society, or for humanity as a whole.

This is another of those subjects where we would need a whole book to explore all the ramifications. The problem is that a man may be required to "give up his life" in ignorance; both being ignorant of why he is doing it and at the behest of ignorant men in power.

How do we judge whether it is worth sacrificing or not?

Can any human being judge what is "right" or necessary for another human being?

It depends on knowing the purpose and "whose" purpose it is.

It depends in "whose name" it is done.

*

The world's "do-gooding" is frequently based on the false premise that man has a will of his own which is directed primarily at survival for its own sake. Our altruism is motivated towards survival of the family or group, the society and perhaps humanity as a whole. The truth is that on a scale less than humanity itself, it

114

inevitably leads to competition and conflict between "expanding" rival groups.

The fallacy of "do-gooding" as commonly promoted and practised is that it totally ignores the *purpose* of human survival.

In the Islamic context, this is to ignore the Will of Allah.

Who knows the destiny of another individual? If you do not know it, how can you possibly help him?

Who knows the destiny of Man?

Could it reasonably be that he should simply survive in peace and procreate *ad infinitum*?

Can Man as a creature know better than Allah what is best for the world?

Inflammatory talk indeed! It would seem that if we follow this to its logical conclusion none of us would lift a finger to help anyone. What a dry, cold, avid world that would be.

The point is that we must be prepared ("made ready before") to help others, and that means abandoning self-will, abandoning pre-conception as to how they may be helped. We do what we understand as being required of us in any given situation without concern for the result. Above all it is done in the knowledge that Allah's Vengeance and His Compassion and Mercy are inextricably interwoven—so much so that they are indistinguishable.

*

History teaches us cycles.

The present moment is a point on the circle, simultaneously a beginning and an ending. Only from the centre may we see the continuing as a whole circle or cycle, the whole story or history.

Thus, for example, we may see that the period of historic time known as the Dark Ages was succeeded by the Renaissance, a flowering of Man's vision and his ability to express and communicate it. The former is described as a period in Western Europe of feudalism (economics based on "slave" labour), of domination by the Roman Catholic Church (the imposition of established religion) and intellectual poverty. Yet it was out of this "restriction"

115

that burst the movement characterized by its emphasis on the individual and the potential evolution of "the complete man". Yet the "seeds" of this fruition were in the Dark Ages themselves, in the secret workings of the mystics and the true alchemists—just as the hidden germination of the seed takes place in the dark of the winter soil, preparing for the seasonal time to break out into the warmth of spring. Phase after phase of the cycle, each one dependent on its predecessor and its successor for its generation and fruition.

Perhaps the deepest scar on the history of our present age is represented by a date: 6th August 1945. On that day the first atomic bomb was exploded over Hiroshima. From that moment Man held in his grasp the possible destruction of the entire species. Man could destroy himself—the ultimate self-destruction. The vengeance of Allah.

What a terrible prospect; what an awful dilemma.

"If only we could put the clocks back." . . . "If only we could wipe the knowledge of the atomic weapon from the mind of man." . . . "If only science had not 'progressed' so far."

If only . . .

Is it a matter of human wisdom?

Do we *really* know what is best for us? And furthermore, did we *really* have any say in what has happened? Before the discovery of atomic power, could we see its consequences and call a halt? Surely not? For, before the discovery—and when did that "start" anymore than when did the "beginning" start—it was there "ahead" of us, in the unknown, waiting for the precise moment of its discovery, inexorably following the consequences of the first blow struck by one human against another.

*

So much of the philosophy of the "do-gooder" (and in that category we embrace the political, the religious, the economic and the humanist credos) is based on the belief that what *should* happen in the future (for the "good" of mankind or the individual) ought to

116

be based *now* on the evidence of what was "good" in the *past*. It would be some kind of Utopia in which all the "bad" ingredients had been eliminated and all the "good" distilled out to create a world of comfort and plenty.

This is the natural, body-identified vision of the fruition of human wisdom which will one day (hopefully) prevail . . . but could Man will it?

But let us take the 6th August 1945 and let us consider it with the heart . . .

Can we, with any honesty, attempt to put the clocks back? Of course we can't.

Are we, truly, disturbed for all those who died in the terrible holocaust? We were not there; we did not experience. Do we now really *experience* anything of the *past*?

Is not our fear that what took place could happen again . . . to us?

Perhaps—just perhaps—that terrible scar is the beginning of "sanity" for the present age; or, perhaps collectively, we have not "learned" from it at all. Perhaps, collectively, man is subject to an inevitable self-destroying madness, if he does not question and understand the real purpose of his existence.

And maybe here is the key. We, you and I, cannot change anything that has happened in the past. And we cannot avoid anything that is going to happen in the future. All we can do as individuals is meet what is happening now and see it, experience it, feel it and understand it to the full depths of our individual being.

Each of us can only observe, question and take into account his own life and death. Each one has to understand the purpose for himself . . . for, collectively, there is no purpose beyond sheer survival.

*

SAY: *He shall give life to them who gave them being at first, for in all creation is he skilled:*
Who even out of the green tree hath given you fire, and lo! ye kindle flame from it.

117

What! must not He who hath created the Heavens and the Earth be mighty enough to create your likes? Yes! and He is the skilful creator. His command when He willeth aught, is to say to it, BE and IT IS. So glory be to Him in whose hand is sway over all things! And to Him shall ye be brought back.

(Surah 60)

Who created the atom bomb?
For what purpose was it created?

*

There are so many reasons for embarking upon a project.

I want something to occupy me; I want something to interest me; I want something to fill my days; I want something to fulfil my desires . . . these are my quest.

There are so many reasons . . .

There are so many ways of engaging with a project.

It may be something you want to do, from time to time . . . like playing golf, or knitting, reading a book, or gardening . . . in other words, a "pastime"; or it may be something that you devote most of your waking hours to . . . like making money, being a success at work . . . in other words, your "occupation".

What is religion to you?

A pastime or an occupation?

At the very outset this question is very important.

If religion is a pastime, then I will probably join a group, attending meetings or services, do certain specific things at specific times— the disciplines or practices of my religion; and the rest of the time I will be unchanged, as I was before I joined the group. My life will only be altered in that I now, occasionally "do" religious things and am occasionally moved or uplifted.

If religion is an occupation with me, it will become my life's work. I will be religious wherever I am and whatever I am doing.

And this is only the start.

If I set out on the flight of the unknown to the unknown I may find myself becoming a member of a religious or philosophical group, but that is only the beginning. In time I will ". . . *ask of his cup-bearer a draught of wine and when I have drunk it nothing else will matter except the pursuit of my true aim.*"

The flight—or journey—must become all important: all else must become of no importance.

*

But how can so many of the things I do be "religious"?
Simply through understanding why I am doing them.
Only then will I be "detached from all that exists".

*

What is my goal? What is my purpose?
Now . . . I ask myself.
What do I really want?
If the answer is any *thing* conceivable, I am in the Valley of The Quest.
Why should it be necessary to become "detached from all that exists"?
Because there is no real purpose in merely existing as a creature. Simply to survive a lifetime on earth is not Man's purpose.
So precarious, so undefined is the path of my flight that if there is anything I want it will deter me; not necessarily for ever—but certainly for a time.
This is a profound fact; all the things of this world distract me from that which lies beyond the veil of mystery; and yet, without the things of this world, how can I conduct myself from day to day, from moment to moment?
I simply attend to them—and, as I fly, they pass by beneath.
Is that not really what we all do all the time?
The memory may sometimes linger, and we may cling to it. But the experience has gone and there is no going back to it.
Is that not, in all honesty, familiar to every one of us?

*

119

What is the point in hanging on to our so-called identity, status and position?

Do we not all play the game of claiming superiority and advantage (or its reverse, the claiming of inferiority and disadvantage)?

If we were honest, would we not admit that we claim knowledge where we do not have knowledge, understanding where we have no understanding and caring where we have no caring?

It is not a comfortable experience to come face to face with *me*— he who plays games and assumes fictional attitudes and attributes far beyond himself (or beneath himself); he who contrives purposes to justify his actions.

The *me* in each of us is continually being distracted by spurious quests, being deluded with beliefs of what it is to be wise, what it is to be kind, what it is to be holy, what it is to tell the truth.

In The Quest it is the wise who admit to themselves that they do not know, yet constantly ask or pray for guidance; it is the kind who admit to themselves that they have no kindness, yet constantly ask or pray to remove their unkindness; it is the holy who admit to themselves that they cannot be holy, yet constantly ask or pray to remember the silent wholeness; and it is the truthful who admit to themselves they cannot tell the Truth, yet constantly ask and pray to realize the untruth.

"Always remember," said Iblis (Satan), "this simple axiom: never say 'I', so that you never may become like me."

*

So:

Here is the Valley of The Quest.

I do not know what I am looking for. I do not know the purpose.

I have only a vague sense of why I am looking for "it".

I believe that only because I am looking for "it", it must be possible for "it" to be found.

I think that activity in mind, manifesting as ceaseless chatter— words—stands between me and the finding.

How far am I prepared to go in my search?

Until I start a journey I have no idea how rigorous it may be.

Of course I must prepare for a journey. I must take adequate food and clothing—and yet, at the same time not over-burden myself with heavy baggage.

I know that I will need all my strength for the journey, but I do not know what may befall me along the way.

I may take quantities of food so that my pack is heavy. I will be glad of that food if I am hungry—but supposing along the way I keep finding food growing that I am able to pick and eat? How foolish I may think to have burdened myself with all the food from home.

'Is it fitting that you should take what is already there? . . . Take then the ardour of love and the longing of the spirit; no one can offer other than this. If a single sigh of love goes to that place it will carry the perfume of the heart . . .'

*

And as the road winds ever onward I may come to a beautiful valley and I may want to stay and live out my days there. And yet I can see the road winding on into the distance. Will I have completed my journey, staying in that valley? I will not have reached the end of the road or could one say that I have reached the end of the road for me? Perhaps there is no end to the road. Our experience of ends—living as we do on a spherical earth mass—is that having gone round the circle we reach the point from which we started. Supposing I go on to "the very end"—and I find myself back where I started! Will it have all been worth while?

That will all depend on the journey.

Our journey is not just a physical journey. Our travel is space travel. Where is the end of space? Am I prepared to give up for ever my earth and travel on deeper and deeper into the unknown; losing sight not only of the physical earth, but of all my subtle recognitions? How do you count time—when there is no day or night? No passing, no aging . . . no birth or death? Who knows? Only by going will I find out!

As we prepare for the journey in the first valley, the Valley of The Quest, it is *me* that has to be disciplined. The "great efforts" are all directed at restoring the natural balance, the "changed state" when *I* and *me* are in their right relationship, the former present, observing and detached, the latter willing and obedient. It is the wilful *me* who "fears the dragons, the guardians of the door", just as it is *me* who has put trust in and held on to "dogma, belief and unbelief".

We may spend a lifetime in the Valley of The Quest . . .

But then, out in Islamic Space, time does not exist, place does not exist.

All the Seven Valleys are contemporaneous and coincident.

As we set out on the flight of the unknown to the unknown the ending will always be the beginning, the arrival will be where we started. Maybe we fulfil the purpose in the journeying itself?

It is all in the seeing and the understanding now.

'*When you enter the first valley . . . a hundred difficulties will assail you . . .*"

but

"*When the door is opened and he enters . . . all cease to exist.*"

V

"In this valley (the Valley of Love) love is represented by fire, and reason by smoke. When love comes reason disappears. Reason cannot live with the folly of love; love has nothing to do with human reason. If you possessed inner sight, the atoms of the visible world would be manifested to you. But if you look at things with the eye of ordinary reason you will never understand how necessary it is to love. Only a man who has been tested and is free can feel this. He who undertakes this journey should have a thousand hearts so that he can sacrifice one at every moment."

(*The Conference of the Birds*)

*

And so the journey has begun. We may not know where it is leading us, nor even where we are leaving from; we know only that we have taken the first step, with purpose.

So it was with our individual births. We none of us knew where we had come from (in "the world's terms"), nor did we know where we were going to (in "the world's terms"); if we "knew" anything at all it was simply that we were alive, experiencing, here *now*.

What did I know as a newly born baby? Of course the question is impossible to answer *now*, because I am no longer that newly born baby and I cannot remember.

But what do I know *now*, born as I am into this present moment? Do I know that I am alive? The snap answer is "Yes"; but is it a truthful answer? What gives me this knowledge of Life? Is it, perhaps, that I am experiencing?

Experiencing what?

If I sit quietly in a chair—what am I experiencing?

At first, the sounds that are all around me; traffic on the road outside, the natural sounds of wind, bird song; my own breathing; the sounds of my body functioning; my clothes rubbing against my skin. It seems that there is no "silence", but a multitude of sounds.

Then the sensations; the weight of my body on the chair; of my clothes against the skin; the air against my face; a slight itching on my scalp; my tongue resting in my mouth; the warmth of my body—and, possibly a sensation of cold if there is a draught, or a pain if part of my body is not comfortable.

Then the smells; of my own body, of the dust in the room, or the flowers in a vase; food cooking, wood burning; all the scents of nature.

The tastes; is there a taste in my mouth? Perhaps the lingering taste of a meal that I have just had; the saliva . . .

And, of course, the sights; if my eyes are open, I see the room in front of me, the play of light on surfaces, tiny particles of dust hanging in a sun ray . . . if my eyes are closed, the warm orange glow of my eyelids, with other indefinable pin-pricks of light that come and go . . .

What am I experiencing?

Life . . . and Love?

*

But *who* is it that is experiencing?

I am.

Therefore I am alive . . . in Life.

If I was not alive—would there be no experiencing?

No, the experience would still be going on—but for other people.

How would I know this?

I wouldn't.

Therefore *I* am something that "drops into" life, experiences and then disappears again?

Experience is a constant while the world and its creatures exist.

"Constant" means that which "stands with".

"Stands with" whom?

That which witnesses it?

If *I* did not hear the sound, taste the flavour, smell the scent, see the image, feel the sensation, would there be any sound, smell, scent, image, sensation?

I am the witness . . . the constant witness.

The "I", the centre of being, in all creatures is *the* witness.

But it is the "spiritual" capacity in Man that may *know* that there is witnessing.

The "I" in you and the "I" in me *knows* the experience of creation.

I know Life . . . and I know Love.

*

For our Life experience is not confined merely to simple awareness of sensory experience. We are also aware of what we have come to term "emotion".

"Emotion: a moving of the feelings: agitation of mind: one of the three groups of the phenomena of mind—feeling, distinguished from cognition and will . . ."

Quite what the emotions *are* is fruitless to enquire. They are, very simply, "an agitation of mind"—as stated in the above dictionary definition.

Rather than wondering how mind can be agitated it would seem more profitable to try to discover *what it is that agitates*.

Love?

*

Love, in all its expressions and guises, is the highest manifestation of the "spiritual way" available to, and experienced by, all people.

When love comes reason disappears . . .

It is Love that makes the warrior into a poet and the poet into a warrior.

Love holds more sway over the minds of men and women than any other experience.

Love transforms the view of things.

It is raining—who cares, if you are going to see your loved one?

It is cold—who notices, when you are with your loved one?

Nothing is too hard, too painful, too difficult for a lover.

But what *is* Love?

Here is a story from "The Conference of the Birds":

A Khoja sold all that he possessed—furniture, slaves and every-thing, to buy beer from a young beer-seller. He became completely mad for love of this beer-seller. He was always hungry because if he were given bread he sold it to buy beer. At last someone asked him: "What is this love that brings you into such a pitiable state? Tell me the secret!" "Love is such," he replied, "that you will sell the merchandise of a hundred worlds to buy beer. So long as you do not understand this, you will never experience the true feeling of love."

*

So, again, what *is* "love"?

Perhaps we could as well ask, "What is pain?", or "What is happiness?"

Pain is a sensation, experienced through the nerves of the body, in the brain. It is caused by a number of different reasons. Pain denotes some imbalance in the body. But what is the pain itself? It is an electric impulse conveyed from that part of the body that is out of the norm, through the nerves, to the brain . . . I still don't know what pain *is*.

Pain cannot be intellectually *known*. It can only be *felt*. Once felt, you know the feeling.

What is happiness?

Happiness is a sensation in the mind of well-being, of content-ment, of peace. It apparently arises for any number of different reasons. Happiness denotes a balance in the psyche. But what is happiness itself? It is a feeling in the mind . . . I still don't know what happiness *is*.

Happiness cannot be intellectually *known*. It can only be *felt*. Once felt, you know the feeling.

And here is an important point.

You *know* the *feeling* of pain—you do not like it; so you attempt to avoid having it again.

You *know* the *feeling* of happiness—you like it; so you attempt to maintain it or to retrieve it.

But you do not know what pain *is*, nor do you know what happiness *is*.

And so you come to believe that what gave you pain before will give it again; what gave you happiness before will give it again.

You pursue your belief as to what will give you happiness, you run from your belief as to what will give you pain. You are chasing shadows—for you do not know what either of them are.

We tend to equate love with happiness and hence we pursue it.

And yet, do we not speak of the pain or agony of love?

*

"The next valley is the Valley of Love. To enter it one must be a flaming fire—what shall I say? A man must himself be fire. The face of the lover must be enflamed, burning and impetuous as fire. True love knows no after-thoughts; with love, good and evil cease to exist . . ."

(*The Conference of the Birds*)

*

Could it then be that all emotion, all disturbance of the mind, is the working of Love?

All our desiring, craving, fearing, affection, competing, acquiring, idolizing, hating, anger . . . is an expression of the Love in us seeking resolution?

All our inertia, apathy, indifference, depression . . . is an absence of Love in us?

Love unites.

Love destroys the illusion of aloneness, separation, incompleteness.

Love *will* not be gainsaid. Allah wills that we shall be united with Him . . . even if we are destroyed in the process.

We may willingly surrender ourselves to Love.

Or we will be wilfully destroyed by Love.

*

Love is being possessed.

It is a question of who or what possesses the being.

At first it will seem that love is caused by the object of love. So one says that a person is possessed by the loved one. It seems as if love comes from the other person; that you are *given* love—and then *feel* it. But you can love someone who does not know you; how can they be giving to someone they do not know? So love is something that you *take* from the other person?

What happens if there is no other person? Can you still "love" without there being another person? You can love things; you can love a house, or a dog, or a tree in the garden. Is that the love of which we are speaking? Does such a love make me a "flaming fire"?

You can love an idea or a principle or an ideal. A political creed or a religious principle can possess you to such an extent that you will go to war, fight and kill for it. Is that the love of which we are speaking?

A person . . . a thing . . . or an ideal . . . all can draw what we call love from us. Or can they?

Sometimes, for a moment, the warm flood of love suffuses the body for no apparent reason; you simply feel "at one" with the world and with yourself. It may only be a momentary experience; you may afterwards find a number of "reasons" why it happened; but at the time it just seemed to "flow through you". Is this the love of which we are speaking?

All love. Love everything . . . tiny sparks of it, flickering flames of it, the furnace of it, the dying embers of it . . . resolving and destroying.

128

Allah's Compassion and Mercy and His Vengeance—all rolled into One.

*

But consider . . .
The flight of the unknown to the unknown.
Who loves?
What is love?
Who or *what* is loved?
If you do not *wholly* and *entirely* desire the far country, then along the way any number of counter-attractions may lure you from the path.

Remember; this quest, this search, this flight . . . is to do with an all-embracing change of life. It is the choice for eternal life rather than habitual death. Because the end is unknown it cannot be looked for.

The *only* possibility of surviving the flight is that you desire the *Simurgh*, or Allah, or Union with the Causal Factor, or call it what you will . . . to the exclusion of all other things. *Including yourself.*

This is Love that is a flaming fire. Fire burns; fire reduces the body to ash; and the ash is scattered on the four winds . . . into the ether, the ethereal Space of Islam.

If my body now is burnt, and my ashes are scattered on the four winds . . . where am I? What has become of *me*?

The "me", the fictional and apparently separate "being" born of "being" identified with the temporal body, becomes the "Being in Love".

The "me" is consumed by Love, the ultimate consummation— the utmost completion —of Love.

May we now glimpse the atomic bomb as the symbol of the Love of Allah? ("Vengeance" derives from roots meaning "proclaim power".)

*

We will all die. It is an unavoidable fact. We will all be meta-phorically scattered to the four winds. The only question that remains is; shall we die knowingly or in ignorance?

The "knowing" or "conscious" death is a "suicide"; a "suicide" for Allah. It is not necessary for the body to be killed for the "suicide" to take place; but the being will be so changed, so transformed, that "good and evil cease to exist".

It all began, in Judaic, Christian and Islamic terms when Adam and his wife Eve ate of the tree of the knowledge of good and evil in the garden of Eden—now the only escape is death, the passing back by way of the "flaming sword which turns every way, to keep the way of the tree of life".

Death, not in ignorance, but through Love; through submission and sacrifice to the Loved One, to the Unknown, the One Nothing.

*

We each of us are given a taste of what it is like to love. But our taste is only the beginning. However, let us be strengthened by it. Anyone who has loved would rather love again. The lover has a sense of wholeness, of holiness. The Love may destroy us, but once it has been experienced then, like one drunk with wine, we are mindless of our safety.

We only want to be united with the Loved One.

He who undertakes this journey should have a thousand hearts so that he can sacrifice one at every moment.

VI

The Hoopoe continued: "After the valley of which I have spoken, there comes another—The Valley of Understanding, which has neither beginning nor end. No way is equal to this way, and the distance to be travelled to cross it is beyond reckoning.

"Understanding for each traveller, is enduring; but knowledge is temporary. The soul, like the body, is in a state of progress or decline; and the Spiritual Way reveals itself only in the degree to which the traveller has overcome his faults and weaknesses, his sleep and his inertia, and each will approach nearer to his aim according to his effort . . ."

(*The Conference of the Birds*)

*

But what *are* my faults, what my weaknesses?

Who can tell me?

This valley, The Valley of Understanding, is to so many the stumbling-block along the way. So many of us falter here and perhaps fall.

What *are* my faults, and *who* can tell me?

Only "I" knows . . .

But can I be understood by *me*?

No: for it is I who must understand.

Understand *what*?

The Truth.

I would stand under the Truth.

*

*

My faults—and I can only speak for myself—are all those things that enchant me along the way . . .

But, of course, we are in Space now; dimensionless Space. Things are not as they are *in earth.*

Once I think I have turned aside (from the Way), drawn by some irresistible impulse to see or to hear, to touch or to taste or to feel . . . once I have turned aside then my new direction is the Way. For Love has taught me that there is no good nor bad in the world's terms.

Wherever *I* am NOW, that is the way, the direct way, the only way to my lover, to the *Simurgh*, to the beginning without end. "I" am the Way itself.

The Valley of Understanding is a "lonely" place—for no one else can understand for me or with me. "I" understand Truth; there is no One else.

*

It is right that the Valley of Understanding follows the Valley of Love—how could it be otherwise? For I need love's chastening fire to reduce *me* to the dust from which understanding only can spring.

There are different ways of crossing this Valley, and all birds do not fly alike. Understanding can be arrived at variously . . .

*

Some it is who may find understanding in a lover's caress, and some in the harsh reminder of the Hiroshima holocaust; some may briefly understand through feeding a baby, and some through a mathematical formula.

Whoever has briefly understood has not reached "the end of understanding"; for there is no end in Truth, nor is there any beginning.

Truth may be likened to light.

The only way that you can "prove" light is through "darkness". If there were no darkness, would there be light?

It is the "untruth" that demonstrates "Truth".

And yet, how can there be, for us, pure "untruth", any more than there can be total "darkness"? Would it not be more correct to say that there are degrees of the lack of light, that there are degrees of untruth? Untruth and truth are relative and degrees of one are the same as degrees of the other.

Consider:

You are about to eat a piece of "bad" meat. I say: "That meat is bad."

True or false? Or relatively true *and* relatively false?

The "bad" meat is then forked into the ground to nourish the soil as manure.

Is the meat then "good" or "bad"?

There is no absolute "good" nor absolute "bad" is there?

There is only the meat in its present state and a series of different conditions pertaining to it.

There is truth-untruth with a small "t". And Truth.

Moral codes tell us that we should "tell the truth".

In Truth, how can we *not* tell the Truth?

We "lie" out of fear. The fear is the Truth.

We "lie" out of selfish desire. The selfish desire is the Truth.

Whatever *is* must be the Truth. How can it *be* otherwise?

The temptation of the Valley of Understanding is that one person may believe he can understand for another, whereas in Truth, it asks each one to understand his own so-called faults and weaknesses.

We must understand "the present state" of ourselves regardless of the worldly "conditions pertaining to it".

If true understanding is "standing under" the Truth, then every one of us is standing under Truth for himself. Our real faults and weaknesses are then simply those beliefs about ourselves that prevent our realizing it to be so.

*

"When the sun of understanding brightens this road each receives light according to his merit and he finds the degree assigned to him in the understanding of truth. When the mystery of the essence of beings reveals itself clearly to him the furnace of this world becomes a garden of flowers. He who is striving will be able to see the almond in its bright shell. He will no longer be preoccupied with himself, but will look up at the face of his friend. In each atom he will see the whole; he will ponder over thousands of bright secrets.

(*The Conference of the Birds*)

*

Only Truth . . . and an infinite number of ways of understanding it.

In the Valley of Understanding—we must understand "understanding". That is all. For with "understanding" we grow obedient to our capabilities, our "gifts", our basic make-up. Don't ask the mathematician to feel with the hands of a potter; nor the musician to see with the eyes of a painter.

Each to his own; each tiny fraction of us, making up the Whole. One Whole. If one particle of the Whole changes—then the nature of the Whole is changed . . .

In the Valley of Understanding "I" am alone; but in the Valley of Understanding "I" am essential; for "I" am the mind of God.

*

"But, how many have lost their way in this search for one who has found the mysteries! It is necessary to have a deep and lasting wish to become as we ought to be in order to cross this difficult valley. Once you have tasted the secrets you will have a real wish to understand them. But, whatever you may attain, never forget the words of the Qur'an, 'Is there anything more?' . . ."

(*The Conference of the Birds*)

*

Is there anything more?

For as long as there is a question in the mind, the answer must be "Yes".

There is no end to understanding; for to Under-stand is to be at the beginning and to Know the place for the first time; to Under-stand, is to stand immediately under Truth, and to be at one with Truth, to be . . . always . . .

. . . changed and yet un-changed; the same and not the same; the beginning that is never ending . . . the ever-continuing *now*.

*

Is this all a dream and an illusion?

Is it all "poetic nonsense"? A flight . . . but merely of fancy?

Can we verify it for ourselves?

In "The Conference of the Birds", the Hoopoe (the bird that is guide to all the other birds on their journey to the *Simurgh*) places the Valley of Love immediately before the Valley of Under-standing.

Through Love we Understand with the heart in a way that we can never know with the mind. It is this "feeling knowledge" of the heart that is essential to us as we journey out into space.

We have to "give up" or sacrifice all our logical thinking to the feeling of the heart; but that is not enough in itself. If the heart is left in control, we will never be free . . . for it is attracted and binds itself to many things.

At first we are the captive of our thinking; but the greater and more ancient captivity—when we come to see it—is the captivity of the emotions. All heart and no head makes for a very erratic companion!

When in doubt, listen to both!

Let the head guide our searching; let the heart understand our feeling.

See how the balance begins to level out as the two are made one within the traveller.

The head and the heart in balance, each doing its own work,

neither dominating the other . . . the head guiding and the heart understanding.

Too much heart in the head—and we are "hot headed" . . .

Too much head in the heart—and we are "cold hearted" . . .

Just the right balance and we will cross the third valley, the Valley of Understanding.

We will not then say, "I understand such-and-such a fact", or "I understand so-and-so", or "I understand some thing"; such illusion will belong to the long ago and the far away.

What we will say as we reach the farther range of the mountains of uncertainty that edge the Valley of Understanding is, "I am", (heart-felt), and "I know I am" (head-known).

And that will be understanding and Understanding will be; for in that moment Truth begins to reveal Itself.

And, in Truth, who then am I?

*

A number of versions exist of a story concerning one of Muhammad's followers called Bilal, a negro slave. For his disobedience, his Meccan master beat, imprisoned and then staked him out in the desert, exposed to the heat of the sun, with a great stone crushing his chest. Through his suffering he would not deny his faith and, during his dying gasps, kept uttering: "One! One! One!"

VII

'Then comes the Valley of Independence and Detachment where there is neither the desire to possess nor the wish to discover. In this state of the soul a cold wind blows, so violent that in a moment it devastates a vast space: the seven oceans are no more than a pool, the seven planets a mere spark, the seven heavens a corpse, the seven hells broken ice. Then, an astonishing thing, beyond reason! An ant has the strength of a hundred elephants, and a hundred caravans perish while a rook is filling his crop . . ."

(*The Conference of the Birds*)

*

Fact or fiction?

Which is which in our experience?

"Fiction" we say, "is based on fact."

But is not fact equally based on fiction?

We learn "facts". We are taught many things and we believe them to be true. We can rely on "fact". And, so long as the head dominates and the heart is ignored, we can live by the "facts" because they seem consistent, and provable by the senses, within the laws of the three-dimensional space-time continuum.

A chair is "a chair" because that is the name I learned to give it. A chair is there because it is "solid" and I can touch it.

Two plus two equals four is a fact. I was taught to recognize one object as separate from another and learned the concept of them being "two". Two separate objects and then two more separate objects; that I call "four"; and so long as I rely on identifying separate objects two of them plus two more of them will consistently and lawfully make four of them. Thus I build my world of "facts" and judge them true.

But there must have been a time when there was no such thing as a chair and no one had ever counted separate objects. Someone must have invented those names and numbers. Does that not mean that those "facts" began as "fiction"?

This the heart knows and after the first experience of love—love consuming, love engulfing, love suffusing—I begin to see the fiction of fact emerging with increasing intensity.

What is a chair? A name for some pieces of wood put together in a certain shape. What is wood? Dead tree? A gathering together of millions upon millions of whirling atoms? What is an atom?

What is "two"? Is it anything? What is a number? A plurality, of what? One? How can there be more than one one? "Two ones" is impossible, since, if there is one, there cannot be another.

'I love you," we say. Who is it who loves? What is love? Who is it who is loved?

"Irritating games!" mind will say. "It is all perfectly obvious. The fact is that a chair is a chair, two plus two equals four and I love you. If we complicate everything by questioning its very basis, we shall be in doldrums of uncertainty."

If we wish to remain "earth-bound", relying and putting our trust in the "facts of life", so be it . . .

*

But it is in the experience of emotions or feelings that the illusion of fact can be most clearly discerned.

Emotions change like the weather.

That which I love today, I may hate tomorrow; that which I desired yesterday, I may ignore today.

It is as though the emotions, as their name implies, are always in motion and such change is in opposition to the stability of fact.

What is fact or fiction, true or false in the continual rise and fall of the emotions? What is stable in the world of feelings?

If love can come and go—is love a fact or a fiction?

Again we must ask ourselves; *who* loves?

Do *I* love—or is it *me*?

"Me" cannot love. "Me" desires to be loved. "Do you love me?"

"I love" has the quality of *giving*; "me" can only *take* love.

For as long as we *take* love, reach out for it, search for it, and, believing that we have found it, take it and claim it and "make it mine", then, for that time, we must suffer the rise and fall, the coming and going, the flowering and withering of the "affections". (What an apt word; for we are indeed *affected*.)

"I love" is a giving but the moment we identify and name the object of our love—"I love you"—we, in turn become subjective. This can so often beg a confirmation from the beloved—"And I love you".

"I love you" says "Please, you love me."

But "I love" or "I am in love"—these can be unconditional giving and unconditional being.

The Valley of Independence and Detachment.

"Then comes the valley where there is neither the desire to possess nor the wish to discover . . ."

What a wonderful possibility: to experience all the revitalization, all the surge of energy, all the liberation from the mundane, that "loving and being in love" releases—while at the same time being free of the pitfalls, the snares and delusions, of naming the *object*, of relying on and making the object responsible for love. Thus is avoided the disillusionment of losing one's love, of being "out of love", of being "unloved".

Just "I love" and "I am in love". No idol. Just a state of giving and a state of being.

I love. Alone. All One.

Like standing alone in a desert, surrounded by an expanse of sand and sky; alone . . . picture it . . . you and . . . what? As far as you can see in any direction, an infinite horizon. Above you the blue beyond . . . around you, as far as the eye can see, undulating sand-banks . . . soft gold and hazy-white . . . beneath your feet,

139

parched earth, depth upon depth. You are *alone* in a wilderness.
By day a savage sun beats down, by night cold winds . . .

You are alone . . . in the wilderness.

It is . . . bewildering.

Who sees you?

Who knows that you are there?

Who cares?

*

When you fall, what supports you? Only the sand.

When you walk, where are you going? Across the sand.

When you die, what will cover you? An immensity of sand . . .

*

This is the nature of the fourth valley.

"*In this valley nothing old or new has value; you can act or not act.
If you saw a whole world burning until hearts were only shish kabab,
it would be only a dream compared to reality . . .*"

*

Why finish writing this book?

Why continue to read it?

We are surrounded by a vast space; blue above, golden beneath,
fading to bleached-white at the rim . . . Where are we going?
Where?

From the cradle to the grave?

From darkness to light?

From Iblis to Allah?

Where?

Only the sun beats down, harsh and unyielding.

"*If myriads of souls were to fall into this boundless ocean it would
be as a drop of dew. If heaven and earth were to burst into minute
particles it would be no more than a leaf falling from a tree; and if
everything were to be annihilated, from the fish to the moon . . .*"

*

Above all else, in our present experience of life, we avoid speculation as to the possible valueless-ness of things; for if we cease to trust in "things" how can we conduct ourselves?

If we are alone in an expanse of sand—all alone—who sees us? We cannot see ourselves. What is there to see? A sameness surrounds us. Where are we going? As far as the far horizon—there is nothing but sand.

"*In the name of Allah, the Compassionate, the Merciful*" becomes a reality when I am thrown into a situation where I am (or appear to be) entirely alone.

Ultimately I "pray" because there is no one to speak to; and in praying, to whom am I speaking?

Who hears when, all alone, I speak? Only I.

Who am I?

*

"*If there remain no trace of either men or jinn, the secret of a drop of water from which all has been formed is still to be pondered over.*"

*

In the fourth valley, the Valley of Independence and Detachment, "a cold wind blows."

We do not choose such detachment, we do not seek such independence—it comes as reality through the Will of Allah. Only the strong can survive it. For in this Valley, there is only God—and to pray is to hear yourself praying.

What can you ask for—when you want no thing nor believe in any thing?

You pray only for compassion, only for mercy . . . not for life, nor for death; not to survive, nor for the journey to cease; only that the Will of Allah be done.

Pray *for* something—any thing—and you are praying for youself.

When you give up *the desire to possess and wish to discover*, then, and only then, are you ready to pray:

Praise be to Allah, Lord of the worlds!

Praise to the unknown, unprovable . . .
The Compassionate, the Merciful!
Blind faith? Or, for as long as I survive, the only invocation?
King on the day of reckoning!
For, without such an acknowledgement, *I* would be supreme, and how can *I* trust that idea—surrounded as I am by the be-wilderness?
Thee only do we worship, and to thee do we cry for help.
Alone, and yet not alone; *I* hear the voice *I* speak.
Guide Thou us on the straight path.
Surrounded as I am by a bewildering desert, where is the path, when all the ground is a path?
The path of those to whom Thou hast been gracious; with whom Thou art not angry, and who go not astray.

*

"Alone in the desert", five times a day, a Muslim kneels towards Mecca and utters the Arabic words of which the above prayer is a translation.

Why? Is it a superstition? Is it a habit?

Yes; perhaps for many Muslims it is.

But for us, on our journey into space, it takes on another, curiously poignant quality if we pause for a moment.

I am sitting in a room, in a town in England; I am surrounded by good friends; in no way could I be compared to an Arab alone in the desert.

But am I not alone in reality? Are we not each of us alone?

However close I may be to someone . . . I was born alone, I will die alone and my journey through this life will be experienced *alone*.

The Valley of Independence and Detachment is not a place where we *acquire* a state of mind; no, it is the place where we come face to face with what has always been. For as long as I believe in *my* body, *my* mind, and *my* soul—I will be alone, as a separate and vulnerable mortal.

Consider:

Is a drop of water *alone*?
Where is the drop of water in the river or the ocean?
How big is a drop of water?
What is a drop of water?
What am I?
How big am I?
Where am I in nature or in Man?
Am I alone?

*

In the Valley of Independence and Detachment, am I alone?
There are no comparable states. There are no facts. There are no criteria with which to judge anything, once all the fiction has dissolved. I love and I am in Love. There is no measurable period of time, no measurable size or distance. The ant can have the strength of a hundred elephants.
When I am alone as the subject, and the mirage of "me" has been dispelled, I am both the centre and the circumference.
I am alone as All One.
Who am I?
Naked now, stripped of pretension, the mind independent and detached, the question cries out.
Who is asking who he is?
The call of the unknown to the unknown . . .
I am, I answer.

*

"*A pupil demanded an answer from his master to an idle question. The shaikh said : 'First wash your face. Can the perfume of musk be smelled in the odour of putrefaction? I do not impart knowledge to drunken men.'* "

(*The Conference of the Birds*)

VIII

The Hoopoe continued : "You will next have to cross the Valley of Unity. In this valley everything is broken in pieces and then unified. All who raise their heads here raise them from the same collar. Although you seem to see many beings, in reality there is only one—all make one which is complete in its unity . . ."

(*The Conference of the Birds*)

*

And now, in an instant, we pass beyond the limits of ordinary mind; which is to say, the mind conditioned to believe in "facts" can no longer explain or justify experience in the world's terms.

Mind becomes aware of The Quest through questions; mind admits the possibility of Love through acknowledgement of aloneness, incompleteness and ignorance; mind desires Understanding through fear of the unknown; mind even glimpses Independence and Detachment when it feels the cold wind of reality in the unfamiliar, far reaches of its kingdom.

But in the Valley of Unity the sense of separation dies; for ordinary mind to try to understand pure unity . . . we would as well ask a living being to describe what lies in wait beyond the grave.

*

Why?

There are words in our vocabulary that define and describe the sense of unity—oneness, single, singular, individual, undivided, and so on. If there are such words, and we assume we know what they mean, why is it so difficult to enter the Valley of Unity, to become unified?

If I contemplate the concept of unity, my mind conceives of it. I conceive of it "out there"; I project it as being "outside" or "beyond" *me*; there is unity apart from *me*. Me *and* unity? Impossible. Me *and* Allah? Impossible.

The drop of rainwater falling onto and merging into the ocean is united with the Whole. There is no drop of rainwater *and* the ocean of water, existing as two separate bodies; there is only "water". Either "water" compounded of an infinite number of drops of rain, or One "water", in the ocean, in the air . . . everywhere.

That is unity—as expressed by water.

But Pure Unity includes *me*—therefore *me* cannot comprehend Pure Unity.

Although you seem to see many things, in reality there is only one—all make one which is complete in its unity . . .

*

You may take a lighted candle to light another candle.

One flame, and then two flames.

But where did the first flame come from?

And where does it go to if you blow it out?

No flame; one flame giving rise to the possibility of an infinite number of flames; coming from nowhere, going nowhere; sometimes here, sometimes there; all the seeming separate manifestations of Flame, the One Flame.

So with Love; coming from nowhere, going nowhere; sometimes here, sometimes there; all the seeming separate manifestations of Love, the One Love.

So with Life . . .

*

This is a most profound moment.

We have reached the limit of "separate-thinking" mind.

What must we do?
Stay still and observe.
Rest, and feel what the heart knows.

*

"There is me, and there is you," conditioned mind is saying, "two separate bodies, looking at each other. You can turn away from me now and leave my sight. You can go about your own business, doing things that I am not even aware of, experience the world a hundred, a thousand, a million miles from me . . . and yet we are One?"

Or, because my mind wants to understand and is also (and this is very important) persuaded that the mind of Farid Ud-Din Attar, the author of "The Conference of the Birds", knows more than my mind does, my mind may try a more subtle evasion, saying:

"When I am dead, where do I go to? Before I was born, where did I come from? Before birth and after death, then there is Pure Unity. I see it clearly; of course all living beings come from no where, all living beings are going no where. There is Pure Unity, *outside* life. Indeed, if you follow the argument through, where did water come from *originally*, or any thing. Yes. It is all *before* creation or *after* creation . . . not here and now, but in some other place and at some other time."

And explaining-and-justifying-mind, relieved, settles back once more with the familiar, another incomprehensible resolved!

Why is mind relieved? Because for a moment there, faced by the awe-fulness of Pure Unity, it contemplated a challenge it could not accept. It saw what was for me the verge of madness, the ghost of suicidal death.

The mind is conditioned to protect me, as well it should . . . until I am prepared to love unconditionally.

*

But what of the heart?
Attar tells a story in the Valley of Pure Unity:

A young woman fell into a river, and her lover jumped in to save her. When he reached her she said: "Oh, why do you risk your life because of me?" He said, "For me there exists no other person than you. When we are together then truly I am you and you are me. We two are one. Our two bodies are one, and that is all."
When duality disappears, unity is found.

*

But, my mind argues, if the young woman and the lover are One, how could she fall into the river and he not? Or, she having fallen in, why follow her? They are One, he can never lose her. Ah, yes; an arm is part of the body, but you can lose an arm . . . but you are not then the same body . . .

Be silent mind; be silent.

Submit . . .

Surrender . . .

Islam . . .

O

O my heart

O my heart, if you wish to arrive at the beginning of under-standing . . .

*

Silent mind . . .

Open heart . . .

Vulnerable and naked, unprotected, with neither the desire to possess nor the wish to discover . . .

The voyager is now exhausted, neither able to go on nor to turn back . . .

Only the longing remains.

But the longing for what? For any thing at all?

Mind is helpless. It can make no more efforts to comprehend. It isn't a case anymore of having to believe or not having to believe.

There is only the infinitely fine, piercing, painful ecstasy of longing itself.

147

Longing . . . to belong? . . . longing to be? . . . longing to be united?

Is it then that the mind must simply and one-pointedly surrender itself to the longing . . . submit unconditionally to the longing, not knowing whose longing it is?

Its sense of separateness will be consumed . . . and beyond is unknown. But did we not say that the known is a fiction? The Unknown, the Islamic Space is as Nothing. Nothing is undivisible and therefore Unified.

Could we have faith that it is the Reality?

Mind! How can you know?

It is sheer frustrated exhaustion that grinds mind into dust.

How we have abused it; how the heart overflows with compassion for it—"poor mind, staked out on the sands of bewilderment . . ."

NO!

STOP!

It is through MIND that these words are being thought; this is all an illusion. Nothing is taking place. I can stand up now, go into the next room, make a cup of tea . . .

*

Can a book ever tell you? Can a book make you taller, more beautiful, change your being?

If you recognize validity in a book—was not that validity already within *you*?

If you do not recognize anything in the book; is the book "wrong", or are you "wrong"?

To be consumed by the overwhelming longing of Pure Unity is a lifetime's work; it is not something that you learn from the pages of a book. The book can only confirm what you already suspected.

*

Even Attar experienced difficulties describing the mysterious Valley of Unity.

148

And now, O Attar, leave your metaphorical discourses and return to the description of the mysterious Valley of Unity.

The Hoopoe continued: "*When the spiritual traveller enters this valley he will disappear and be lost to sight because the Unique Being will manifest himself; he will be silent because this Being will speak.*

"*The part will become the whole, or rather, there will be neither part nor whole. In the School of the Secrets you will see thousands of men with intellectual knowledge, their lips parted in silence. What is intellectual knowledge here? It stops on the threshold of the door like a blind child. He who discovers something of this secret turns his face from the kingdom of the two worlds. The Being I speak of does not exist separately; everyone is this Being, existence and non-existence is this Being.*"

*

Even the supplication of prayer ceases to be effective here, where *I* am not. Only the sound remains humming through . . .

In the deepest ecstasy of such prayer, where am I? Am I awake or asleep, here or there?

No where.

Awake in sleep.

O my heart . . .

Listen . . . and go on listening . . . listen . . .

O my heart . . .

O . . .

*

Prayer is not asking God or Allah for some thing; how can it be? We already have all that we require.

Prayer is not telling God some thing; how can it be? There is no thing that He does not know. "His command when He willeth aught is to say to it BE and IT IS".

Prayer is the bridge that dissolves the duality Man *and* God, God *and* Man.

When duality disappears, unity is.

You do not ask to see God, nor wish to know Him. He is, and you are not.

. . . there is neither the desire to possess nor the wish to discover . . .

The silent mind and the open heart . . .

If the mind is silent, where am I?

If the heart is open, who am I?

Prayer, true prayer, is the sound of Allah filling the mind with His Will to the exclusion of all else.

When the mind is full of the sound there is no space left for my *thinking.*

And if there is no thinking, then there is no "I" thinking.

When there is no "I" thinking, there is no "I" hearing the sound.

When there is no "I" hearing the sound, there is no hearing.

When there is no hearing, there is no sound.

When there is no sound, there is no thing.

When there is Nothing, then there is unity.

In this valley everything is broken in pieces and then unified . . .

No me.

No I.

No Man.

No God.

No thing.

UNITY.

"*No one has ever come back into the world who has made this journey . . .*"

IX

After the Valley of Unity comes the Valley of Astonishment and Bewilderment, where one is prey to sadness and dejection. There sighs are like swords, and each breath a bitter sigh; there, is sorrow and lamentation, and a burning eagerness. It is at once day and night. There, is fire, yet a man is depressed and despondent. How, in his bewilderment, shall he continue his way? But he who has achieved unity forgets all and forgets himself. If he is asked: "Are you, or are you not? Have you or have you not the feeling of existence? Are you in the middle or on the border? Are you mortal or immortal?" he will reply with certainty: "I know nothing, I understand nothing, I am unaware of myself. I am in love, but with whom I do not know. My heart is at the same time both full and empty of love . . ."

(*The Conference of the Birds*)

*

What more can be said?

The air is very fine now—it only just sustains.

Are we in a rocket moving through space or flying on the wing across a high, desolate valley?

Am I seated at my desk?

Where am I?

If I stay in the state of Pure Unity, then I . . . "am not".

If I am not—then there is no desk, no writing, no living even.

For as long as I am living I have to return from Pure Unity, cease the praying until the next time . . . I have to go about my daily tasks. I that have been broken in pieces and then . . . unified?

Did any of it happen? As I see the familiar room, and hear the familiar sounds and smell and taste and touch in the three dimensions of existence.

Can both states be present at the same moment?

If you have been in love, and now your lover is taken from you—are you still "in love"? Can you be both "in love" and "not in love" at the same time? When you are "not in love", how can you be in that which you do not have?

Once you have tasted the sweet fruit of love and believe you have lost it, you are like a person who is searching for his spectacles and does not realize that he is wearing them.

Once I have sunk out of sight and have dissolved into the depth of my being—once I have been broken in pieces and then unified—once there has been the experience of my being *absent* and then *returning* . . .

"Here" and "there" do not exist.

The centre *is* the circumference.

The Whole is never other than the Whole.

Allah is All . . . ah!

*

NOW

Sit in a comfortable position, calm and still, empty the mind of all that wearisome "thinking" . . . all that desiring and fearing, all that explaining and justifying.

Ask one question—and listen to it.

Where am I?

Don't listen to those answers—just keep asking the question.

Where am I?

Keep asking:

Where am I?

*

Here? On earth? Where is the earth? The universe? Where is the universe?

Where? In the mind? Where is the mind? In my body? Am I

152

sure? I hear a sound outside in the street. Did the sound come into my mind in my body, or did my attention reach out to the sound in the street?

Where is your mind? In your head? Press your finger nail against your thumb until it hurts. Where are you feeling the pain? In your thumb . . . in your mind . . .?

Where? Where is the centre of my mind? Where the circumference?

*

Eventually the mind surrenders:

"*I know nothing, I understand nothing, I am unaware of myself. I am in love, but with whom I do not know. My heart is at the same time both full and empty of love.*"

*

Like the lemming, I am hurtling towards the cliff-edge of my own destruction.

Can this be *religion*?

Not as it is taught to the initiate!

Allah grant me The Quest.

Allah grant me Love of The Quest.

Allah grant me Understanding of the Love of The Quest.

Allah grant me Independence and Detachment of the Understanding of the Love of The Quest.

UNITY . . . UNION . . .

In the Name of Allah, the Compassionate, the Merciful.

There is only astonishment and bewilderment.

Astonishment . . . the mind struck silent "before the reverberating sound", usually of thunder, the "hammering" of the god who protects mankind from demons.

Bewilderment . . . "be-willed" . . . the mind "lost in pathless places", denied its wilfulness.

Not freedom for *me*, not peace for *me*, not bliss, joy, happiness for *me*.

Not wisdom for *me*.

I do not know anything but the longing, now, as I approach the ending.

And the ending is only the beginning in the continuous circle of Love.

Again I say, "like Icarus with melting wings, I am flying too close to the sun."

But how else may I approach death—not in ignorance—but *knowing death*.

In order to die, I had to be born.

To die Knowing, I have to live.

And, in the ending . . . or the beginning . . . there is only death, the ethereal Space of Islam.

X

The Hoopoe continued: "Last of all comes the Valley of Deprivation and Death, which it is almost impossible to describe. The essence of this Valley is forgetfulness, dumbness, deafness and distraction; the thousand shadows which surround you disappear in a single ray of the celestial sun . . ."

(*The Conference of the Birds*)

*

Death is rarely discussed to much avail—perhaps because so little is known about it! How can the mind describe being dead? No one has ever claimed to know they are dead. No living person can tell you about it from his present experience.

All that can be said with certainty is that each body will exhaust its time of usefulness and disintegrate.

From this side of the grave that means quite simply that the person ceases to exist in what we call "life". The body disintegrates —and may be seen to do so. The mind of the person no longer influences—other than as a lingering memory-image, or through the record of his or her past works.

The person only continues to exist in the minds of other people— and as time passes the memories become blurred and they themselves eventually die.

Meanwhile new beings are being born into this "life" . . .

The process is an ever-moving chain.

Between the birth and the death is the individual lifetime.

A man may spend this lifetime searching for Truth; and another man may want nothing more than to survive his days in comfort and security. Which is the wiser of those two men?

Death, the great leveller, will take them both.

It all depends what your heart wants.

There are not "things" that you *should* want and "things" that you *should not* want, however much it may be suggested there are. That is the world's way.

If you can *really* hear your own sound in the heart then all that is required is the courage to take the first step on the perilous journey that leads the listener into the source of his music, the lover into the beloved, Man into God.

You may hear God in an instant; but to be One in Him will be as long as a lifetime takes.

Then death of the body holds no fear; and no man can judge another man's going, nor how effectively he has lived. His words and deeds in history have nothing to do with what he realized for himself.

We each live to the best of our ability. It is a question of what we have realized during that living. And ultimately that is to know by whose will we have lived.

If I have remained identified with my body, believing I have separate and independent will, then death will be my destruction. But supposing during life it is realized fully that belief in "me" being an autonomous entity is a fiction or an illusion? Supposing I abandon self-will in the realization that there is only the Will of Allah and that all life's happiness and hardship is demonstration of Love?

In surrendering and abandoning "my" separate identity, in forgetting "me", who is there to die?

There can only remain the longing in the heart for the One True Identity.

So glory be to Him in whose hand is sway over all things! And to Him shall ye be brought back.

*

And so, if we take the first step, we shall not fear the judgement of others. We shall not claim or hold on to any of the "things" which attach us to existence. We shall hope to have the courage to be responsible for whatever happens to us. In Islamic terms, this is to "hear" the Will of Allah and in obedience to it to "make your own sound".

You may be persecuted for your love; you may suffer for it; eventually you will certainly die for it; but once you have heard your own sound there is no denying it. Once undertaken, though you may from time to time linger, there is no turning back.

How does one know one's own sound?

It was contained in the first breath you inhaled. That breath opened the heart. It sounded in the first breath you exhaled and has been in your heart ever since. It suffuses your body, it makes you, you. It calls you and it answers your call.

"*I* am" that first sound; and it makes *me*.

*

Full circle we have come and our ending is our beginning. The birth and the death are one, as the pencil completes its curve.

We do not know any of this.

But, perhaps, there is a feeling . . .

*

Let the last words of the second part be Attar's—for he has been our guide into the Unknown.

One night, the moths met together tormented by a desire to be united to the candle. They said: "We must send someone who will bring us information about our amorous quest." So one of them set off and came to a castle, and inside he saw the light of a candle. He returned, and according to his understanding, reported what he had seen. But the wise moth who presided over the gathering expressed the opinion that he understood nothing about the candle. So another moth went there. He touched the flame with the tip of his wings, but the heat drove him off. His report being no more satisfying than the first, a third went out. This one, intoxicated with love, threw himself on the flame; with his forelegs he took hold of the flame and united himself joyously with her.

He embraced her completely and his body became as red as fire. The wise moth, who was watching from afar off, saw that the flame and the moth appeared to be one, and he said: "He has learnt what he wished to know; but only he understands, and one can say no more."

*

O my heart . . .

Part Three

At last thou hast departed and gone to the
*   Unseen;*
'Tis marvellous by what way thou wentest from
*   the world.*
Thou didst strongly shake thy wings and feathers,
*   and having broken thy cage*
Didst take to the air and journey towards the
*   world of the Soul.*
Thou wert a favourite falcon, kept in captivity by
*   an old woman:*
When thou heard'st the falcon-drum thou didst fly
*   away into the Void.*
Thou wert a love-lorn nightingale among owls:
The scent of the Rose-Garden reached thee, and
*   thou didst go to the Rose-Garden.*

(*Thou Didst go to the Rose-Garden*, Jalalu'd-Din Rumi)

*

A man stands alone in the desert.

Beneath his feet the parched and shifting sand, stretching away from him to the limits of his vision. Above him, by day, a blazing sun, set in a vault of ethereal blue; by night, a thousand glimmering stars in the darkness of the sky.

Suppose, just suppose, that the man has no memory of the past of his life . . . or that there has ever been another man on earth before him.

And suppose, just suppose, that he cannot imagine a future of his life.

159

Because there is no past for him, there cannot be any future.
Because there is no memory, there is no imagining.
Caught at the centre, surrounded by the unknown . . .
What does he think?
What does he say to himself?
What supports his continuing life?

*

A man stands alone on the surface of another planet—an alien world.

He is not sure what is beneath his feet—some substance, which has not been given a name, stretching away to the limits of his vision. Above him in the dark vault of space hangs suspended a moon-like planet—his earth home.

Suppose, just suppose, that he has no memory of his past life . . . no memory that he ever belonged to that other world.

And suppose, just suppose, that he cannot imagine a future of his life in this unfamiliar territory.

Because there is no memory of things past, there is no recognition of things present, no imaginings of things to come.

Caught at the centre, surrounded by the unknown . . .
What does he think?
What does he say to himself?
How does he continue?

*

Just suppose . . .
A baby is born into this world.

At that moment of birth the baby is alone, surrounded by the unknown, the unfamiliar; there is no past for it, in its present form, and, being no past, there can be no imagined future. The unknown is not fearful—because the baby does not even know that it is unknown.

We were each of us just such a baby. I was a baby. You were a baby.

We once, each of us, experienced the bewildering desert and the alien planet. It is in our experience.

Then we began to learn. We became accustomed. The world became familiar.

Without knowing how it happens, we learn to accept that we are here. This is "home" for us—it is as if there had never been any other place.

Once accustomed and familiar, we get on with surviving in our world, attracted to what we learn to be the comforting, recoiling from what we learn to be threatening.

And we grow to forget that we are each alone in an alien place.

The performance of living is so fascinating. There is sleeping and waking, eating and drinking, loving and hating, caressing and fighting, laughing and crying, humans being born and humans dying . . . all familiar, all ordinary, happening to all human beings together; and, most important, happening to me.

What magic cast this spell of familiarity?

Being here in this world is so astonishing and bewildering when you pause to consider it.

What persuades me that what I am doing from day to day has anything more to it than illusory, man-devised meaning and purpose?

Is it some kind of dream?

Is it a madness and chaos which man, who is the only known creature to be conscious of being here, has to believe as having some meaning?

All manner of other people come and go in my life; I do not even know what they feel, what they think, what they see; how was I ever persuaded that I was other than alone?

Supposing I imagine myself the man in the desert, with no memory as to where he has come from nor any image as to where he is going.

Supposing I imagine myself the man stepping on to an alien planet somewhere in space, facing the totally unknown.

In the reality of my present situation here and now, is it any different?

Of course I am with others, and I remember the things I did yesterday, and I am busy today, and I expect to have to do things tomorrow. But who came here with me, who continues with me, and what has all my doing accomplished in any lasting and real terms?

This may be a line of thought that, fearfully, I would prefer not to pursue . . . but then I will never truly turn to Allah unless I do.

*

But do I want to turn to Allah?

Probably not—while all is going reasonably well with me; while I am believing the dream and enjoying the illusion.

For as long as we find the world an enchanting place, we will not want to leave it nor change it. It is only when our plans start to go awry, when we do not get what we want, when we are disappointed . . . when we are unhappy, that we cast about for a way out of our situation.

Thou wert a love-lorn nightingale among owls . . .

Or, perhaps you are sublimely happy where you are. The world is good, you do not expect too much and, therefore, are never disappointed . . . you are not unhappy. Until, quite unexpectedly, you get a glimmer, a sense, a feeling of . . . you know not what, and having been perfectly content where you are, you now begin The Quest for the Unknown.

The scent of the Rose-Garden reached thee, and thou didst go to the Rose-Garden . . .

In either case, once The Quest has begun, really begun, the truth of your being alone begins to dawn.

Let us make no mistake about this, the flight of the unknown to the unknown is a perilous journey because you come to understand —and face up to the realization—that *you do not know anything.*

162

You are alone, unknowing, relying neither on the past memory nor on the future imaginings which have served your worldly life.

Like a fly trapped in amber you struggle to be free.

> Thou didst strongly shake thy wings and feathers
>   and having broken thy cage
> Didst take to the air and journey towards the
>   world of the Soul . . .

From the moment that "the scent of the Rose-Garden" reaches you, you are on your individual flight.

Books such as this one may comfort you for a while, because you realize that you are in the company of like-minded human beings, but, in the end, it is *you* who have to make the flight, the journey—call it what you like—in your own experience.

You are on your own flight.

From that moment we are no longer satisfied with intellectual exercises and diversions nor with emotional appeals and compensations. We are no longer content listening only to one another; a new voice is being heard; the voice is the voice of Allah, of God, of the Unknown . . . the receiving of the voice is entirely individual.

What is it that we are listening to?

How can we be sure that we are being "true to our own sound"?

We are alone on a journey—on what can we rely?

*

> Be silent that the Lord who gave thee language
>   may speak,
> For as He fashioned a door and lock, He has
>   also made a key.

(Be Silent, Jalalu'd-Din Rumi)

*

It is here that I touch on the heart of Islam . . . for the Islamic faith religion offers Five Pillars of support.

Historically and existentially, of course, the religion of Islam is "out there" and its Five Pillars are represented by enacted religious practices that the aspirant must learn and must obey. But psychologically, in the truly Islamic experience of realizing the "being alone in dimensionless space, the unknown", and surrendering all claim and attachment to the existing and familiar, the Five Pillars become the only support on the journey—not as man-devised expedients—but as five principles which we will inevitably have to realize within our own minds in order to steer a stable and sane course through the lifetime of our bodies.

It is in this sense that we may come to understand the Qur'an as the manifestation of "God's eternal and uncreated word". It represents the Eternal Truth—as expressed in relative terms by the man Muhammad at a certain historical time in a certain geographical situation. In Truth, the "uncreated word" is working continuously in each and every man, so that each man is inevitably manifesting "his own Qur'an" or personal recital of his experience, which is why each man is truly "infallible".

How can any man err in being what he is?

*

The first principle I will have to understand is represented by "God is the only God; Muhammad is God's Messenger".

As a religious practice for the Muslim this attestation is repeated continually throughout life.

As a psychological principle, it represents mindfulness that this person here, "me", is subject to Allah, the Absolute Factor, as is every single form in its inter-action with any other form. I, as a supposedly separate entity, have no will. All Will is Allah; and the Whole is Allah.

Allah is therefore the only Allah.

But how do "I", the core of this being, come to realize that "God is the only God"? The realization of it in mind requires that I am informed of it. Who tells me? "Muhammad". Not the historical man—but the same "messenger" of knowledge or understanding

164

which informs every atom of the universe and which once expressed it through the words of Muhammad.

It is "Muhammad in me" who reveals Allah's Will.

How can I be other than I am? How can I err in what I am?

What I am is Allah's Will.

Through "Muhammad in me", I am and I know that I am.

The realization of this first principle is the keystone of my life. Everything else depends on it for its meaning.

How can this person here be alone . . . when it is understood that it is All One?

*

The first pillar is the one on which to base the whole conduct of a lifetime.

The second pillar is worship.

As a religious practice for the Muslim, worship takes the form of a ritual session of prayer five times daily. These prayers, including verses from the Qur'an, are said individually, a personal communion with Allah. If said in the company of others, say in a mosque, the group will have a leader, the *imam*, but he is a co-ordinator, as it were. He is not to be thought of as a priest or intermediary because Islam, as we have suggested in so many ways, is the *direct* surrender of the self to Allah.

As a psychological principle of religiousness, as opposed to a manifest practice, worship means "worth-ship" and indicates the need of the mind to be reminded to submit over and over again, abandoning self-will in order to be "worthy" of fulfilling the Will of Allah.

And the self-will is that which stands between me and Truth. For in Truth I am the Will of Allah and the daily experience of worship is the sense of wonder experienced by me through nature and creation. The scent of a rose will fill the mind and flood the heart. Every breath is a prayer, if it can be recognized. The sound of the wind in the trees can, for a moment, release me from my bondage.

165

Worship is any moment of communion—or "coming into union"; and in that moment the duality is dissolved.

*

The third pillar is almsgiving.

As a religious practice in Muslim society, this means literally giving away a portion of one's wealth to meet the needs of the less fortunate.

Psychologically, it represents the principle in which the true aspirant realizes that in no real sense does he possess anything. Not only does he have to forego any claim, which would be self-willed, but attachment to any "possession" (including beliefs, attitudes and opinions) prevents "detachment from all that exists". All has to be sacrificed, in self-denial, in order for there to be Union in the Divine.

*

The fourth pillar is fasting.

As a performed and literal practice, fasting applies mainly to the annual celebration of Ramadan, the ninth month of the Muslim lunar year. It is a physical discipline of self-denial and purification of the blood.

Psychologically, it again represents self-denial and purification but at the level of disciplining the mind, abstaining from all mental indulgences, a kind of suspension of activity, a regular period of meditation, which allows head and heart to come into balance. Again this purification dissolves self-will and self-love, admitting Will and Love.

*

Finally, the fifth pillar is pilgrimage.

In practice, this is represented by the once-in-a-lifetime obligatory journey of the Muslim to Mecca—historically the focal point of Islam.

Psychologically, it represents the "journey" . . . the journey to

166

the *Simurgh* . . . The Quest for Truth . . . the flight of the unknown to the unknown, which must be undertaken before death if dying is to be conscious.

Pilgrimage is the purpose of life itself. It is life. For a pilgrimage is not only reaching your destination, it is the journey itself.

*

As I set out and travel my lifetime in this mysterious existence, these are the five pillars I need for stability and sanity . . .

The Five Pillars of Islam.

Acknowledgement of and faith *in* God, the One God, the Absolute, Unknown and Omnipotent Factor, Allah.

Worship . . . whereby the mind is made worthy for Love.

Almsgiving . . . whereby the mind is willing to give in response to need.

Fasting . . . whereby the mind abstains from ignorant, indulgent and wilful activity.

Pilgrimage . . . whereby the Self, the "I", obedient to the longing in the heart, journeys into the Islamic Space to experience the seven valleys on the Way to Truth in Death.

*

I need nothing more than that which I have already been given.

Whoever I am, wherever I am, at whatever time, in whatever circumstances—alone in the desert, or on an alien planet—there is the opportunity to make Truth real in me—to realize.

The Quest for Truth may begin with a question:

Who am I?

Who asks that question? Where does it come from? How does it form in the mind?

What is a question? What is its purpose? Why question?

Who is God?

In Islam the image of Allah is never depicted. How can you paint the face of the unknown?

How can you even know it?

How can you know that there is that which you do not know?
What, or who, is knowing that?
It is all the most wonderful, awe-ful, bewildering enigma.
And yet
when the mind is still . . . fasting,
and when the mind is responsive . . . almsgiving,
and when the mind is yearning . . . worship,
and when the mind is drawn . . . pilgrimage,
then
the mind acknowledges . . .
What?
Mind cannot say . . . it is suffused with light . . . beyond words . . .
Try it.
Still the mind: meditate: seek until you find *your* meditation;
your Way of . . .
stilling the mind,
then
respond to the yearning, allow the drawing to take place . . .
and
listen to your own sound.

*

Who am I?
Who is God?
". . . the flight of the unknown to the unknown . . ."
I s l a m.
The word means "surrender" or "submission"
By whom or what *to* whom or what?
S p a c e.
That which appears to be between one and another.
What space is there between Man and God?

*

The Islamic Space.
The circle . . . is the body.

Within the circle . . . is the mind.
That upon which the circle is drawn, that contains the circle . . .
is the soul.
That which caused the circle to be drawn, which was there before
the circle, is there after the circle . . . Allah

*

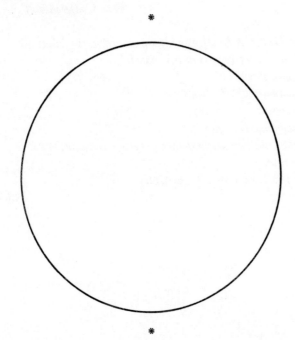

*

O . . . my heart.

Whoso recognises and confesses his own defects
Is hastening in the way that leads to Perfection!
But he advances not towards the Almighty
Who fancies himself to be perfect.

(Jalalu'd-Din Rumi)

The third bird said to the Hoopoe: "I am full of faults, so how shall
I set out on the road? Can a dirty fly be worthy of the Simurgh of the

Caucasus? How can a sinner who turns away from the true path approach the King?"

The Hoopoe said: "O despondent bird, do not be so hopeless, ask for grace and favour. If you so lightly throw away the shield your task truly will be difficult."

(*The Conference of the Birds*)

In the Name of Allah, the Compassionate, the Merciful
O Thou, ENWRAPPED *in thy mantle!*
Arise and warn!
Thy Lord—magnify Him!
Thy raiment—purify it!
The abomination—flee it!
And bestow not favours that thou mayest receive again
with increase;
And for thy Lord wait thou patiently.

(*Surah 74*)